PORTFOL

INDIAN RAILWAYS

BIBEK DEBROY is an economist and is currently a member of Niti Aayog. He was the chairman of a committee set up by the ministry of railways to recommend desired reforms. In the past, he has worked in academia, business chambers and the government. He is the author of several books, papers and popular articles, and writes columns for newspapers and magazines.

SANJAY CHADHA is presently working as joint secretary in the department of commerce where he handles international trade with Northeast Asia. He is also the nodal officer for trade infrastructure and mainstreaming of the Indian states in international trade. He has worked in various capacities for over two decades for the Indian Railways. He done an MBA from the Faculty of Management Studies, University of Delhi and has a bachelor's degree in mechanical engineering and production technology from the Engineering Council, UK. He has published widely in domestic and international journals.

VIDYA KRISHNAMURTHI is a researcher with Indicus Foundation, New Delhi, with an interest and experience in ancient Indian history and cultural history of the premodern period. Her current project focuses on the Indus Valley Civilization and the historical linkages between India and South East Asia. Previously, she worked at Niti Aayog as a Young Professional. She holds a master's in East Asian studies from the Faculty of Social Sciences and a bachelor's in history from University of Delhi. She also writes short stories for children.

GURCHARAN DAS is a world-renowned author, commentator and public intellectual. His bestselling books include *India Unbound, The Difficulty of Being Good* and *India Grows at Night*. His other literary works consist of a novel, *A Fine Family*, a book of essays, *The Elephant Paradigm*, and an anthology, *Three Plays*. A graduate of Harvard University, Das was CEO of Procter & Gamble, India, before he took early retirement to become a full-time writer. He lives in Delhi.

THE STORY OF INDIAN BUSINESS
Series Editor: Gurcharan Das

Arthashastra: The Science of Wealth by Thomas R. Trautmann

The World of the Tamil Merchant: Pioneers of International Trade by Kanakalatha Mukund

The Mouse Merchant: Money in Ancient India by Arshia Sattar

The East India Company: The World's Most Powerful Corporation by Tirthankar Roy

Caravans: Punjabi Khatri Merchants on the Silk Road by Scott C. Levi

Globalization before Its Time: The Gujarati Merchants from Kachchh by Chhaya Goswami (edited by Jaithirth Rao)

Three Merchants of Bombay: Business Pioneers of the Nineteenth Century by Lakshmi Subramanian

The Marwaris: From Jagat Seth to the Birlas by Thomas A. Timberg

Goras and Desis: Managing Agencies and the Making of Corporate India by Omkar Goswami

Indian Railways: Weaving of a National Tapestry by Bibek Debroy, Sanjay Chadha and Vidya Krishnamurthi

THE STORY OF INDIAN BUSINESS

INDIAN RAILWAYS

*The Weaving of
a National Tapestry*

BIBEK DEBROY

SANJAY CHADHA

VIDYA KRISHNAMURTHI

With an introduction by
Gurcharan Das

PORTFOLIO
PENGUIN

PORTFOLIO

USA | Canada | UK | Ireland | Australia
New Zealand | India | South Africa | China

Portfolio is part of the Penguin Random House group of companies
whose addresses can be found at global.penguinrandomhouse.com

Published by Penguin Random House India Pvt. Ltd
7th Floor, Infinity Tower C, DLF Cyber City,
Gurgaon 122 002, Haryana, India

Penguin
Random House
India

First published in Portfolio by Penguin Random House India 2017

Copyright © Bibek Debroy, Sanjay Chadha and Vidya Krishnamurthi 2017
Introduction copyright © Gurcharan Das 2017

10 9 8 7 6 5 4 3 2 1

ISBN 9780143426752

Typeset in Aldine401 BT by Manipal Digital Systems, Manipal
Printed at Replika Press Pvt. Ltd, India

CONTENTS

INTRODUCTION

My heart is warm with the friends I make,
And better friends I'll not be knowing
Yet there isn't a train I wouldn't take,
No matter where it's going.
                              —Edna St Vincent Millay

Every Indian seems to have at least one impossibly romantic railway memory. Mine is of a journey from Kalka to Shimla when I was five. From the window of our train, my family and I feasted, for the first time, on the snow-tipped crests of the Himalayas. With each bend of the winding track, we passed green slope after green slope, their tiers of neatly cultivated terraces looking like gardens hanging in the air. Belts of pine, fir and deodar punctuated the terraces, and masses of rhododendrons clothed the slopes. Below, towards the south, the Ambala plains seemed to recede as the Sabathu and Kasauli hills appeared in the foreground. To the north rose the confused Himalayan mountain chains, range after snowy range.

The train stopped at Barog, where we ate the most delicious *puri-alu*. The station was named after a railway engineer named Barog, who had built the infamous tunnel number thirty-three, as the authors of this volume inform us. He started to dig the tunnel from opposite ends of the mountain, hoping that the digging parties would meet in the centre. But they did not, and Barog shot himself and his dog, unable to bear the ignominy. The railway company then hired a certain Baba Bhalku, who apparently had the ability to tap on the mountain wall with a stick and tell from the sound where it could be dug. Bhalku became a legend and helped to build all the tunnels to Shimla.

One of Bhalku's last tunnels was at Shogi, where we had our first wondrous vision of Shimla. From afar, it looked like a mythical, green-carpeted garden dotted with red-roofed Swiss chalets. My excitement mounted as we neared. We passed Jutogh, crossed Summer Hill, turned into tunnel number 103, and finally reached Shimla's Victorian railway station. By then I had fallen in love with the railway, and ever since, whenever I have heard a train whistle, I have wished, like Edna St Vincent Millay, that I were on that train. But these longings are dying rapidly in an age of railway mediocrity that has crept insidiously upon India during the past two generations.

Indian Railways: The Weaving of a National Tapestry by Bibek Debroy, Sanjay Chadha and Vidya Krishnamurthi is a charming attempt to recapture the power and poetry of the building of, and travel on, the railways in India, from the mid-nineteenth century to Independence. It is hard to imagine that the men who built the railways belonged to a profession of heroes, but this is exactly what our authors show in the lives of engineers like Rowland Stephenson, John Chapman and Arthur Cotton in this lively tenth volume of Penguin's *The Story of Indian Business*. Stephenson dreamt of connecting London and Calcutta by rail, which would reduce the journey between England and its Indian empire to ten days; he also wanted to link Calcutta with Peking and Hong Kong.

Arthur Cotton was a hero to my engineer father. When I was a child, I remember listening to my father speak enthusiastically about Cotton's idea of connecting our subcontinent with inland waterways as an alternative to the railways. To connect India's rivers and form a robust system of inland water transportation was not a hare-brained idea—it was seriously debated in the British parliament in the nineteenth century. The railways won in the end, in part because of a powerful lobby. Ever since, I have nostalgically wondered whether, if India had also invested in inland waterways for transport, we might not have got the side benefit of irrigating our arid lands and making our agriculture less vulnerable while also providing cheap transport to the people. The authors of this book give a fascinating account of this controversy of railways-vs-inland waterways in a dialogue between the anonymous 'P' and 'C'.

The railways brought modernity to India. More than any other product of the industrial revolution—with the possible exception of electricity—the railways affected the very way Indians lived and even thought. They made us suddenly think of class, not caste. By establishing classes of travel—there were more than five passenger classes in pre-Independence India, our authors remind us—we were introduced to the modern usage of 'first class', 'second class', and so on. After Independence, the railways collapsed this social stratification into just two classes. Our caste mindset has not gone away, but it has diminished in urban India. And the railways seem to have played a small part in changing our hierarchical world view.

Imagine how the world must have seemed to the ordinary Indian who had never seen anyone or anything move at a speed greater than fifteen kilometres an hour. The railways liberated us from our narrow, provincial mindset that had been limited to local customs, local knowledge and local connections. They brought us travelling merchants, artisans, singers and new products.

After the 1860s, our horizons began to expand to a world of distant towns and unfamiliar landscapes. And, like the English language, the railways helped to unify India and give us an Indian 'world view'. They changed our public spaces. Major Indian cities were reshaped around railway terminuses, with broad avenues leading up to them. Indeed, the new stations, not only in the metropolitan cities of Calcutta, Bombay, Delhi and Madras, but also in many other cities, brought about a revolution in architecture and urban design in the country.

For the first time, we faced the significance of the railway timetable. Our daily lives began to become time-bound. If our pre-modern world had been space-bound

INTRODUCTION　　　　xi

and time-free, our modern world became space-free but time-bound. The towns and villages that were on the railway line were lucky; they prospered. The others got left behind. The train platform was such a psychological draw that young people went out in the evenings to the platform for chai or *paan,* or merely to linger there for a whiff of modernity. This must have been one of the reasons why 'platform tickets' came into being.

It's easy to forget that train travel was once a romantic adventure. My memory of the Kalka-Shimla Mail came hurtling back to me only after I read Satyajit Ray's crime thriller, *Incident on the Kalka Mail.* A journey by train was an existential distillation of life itself, a glide through time and space, tugged along by an engine that could not be seen but could only be suggested by the trails of smoke in its wake. I can still hear the roar of the steam engine and the turn of the wheels of the Kalka-Shimla train, and I am ready to go.

~

The story of Indian railways, we learn from this book, began in London in the 1840s. The promoters were adventurous, determined men. They got in touch with Britain's merchants, manufacturers and shipping interests, to whom they held out the prospect of a vast and opulent India. Once opened up by railways, they said, India would become a fabulous supply house of cotton and wheat, and a huge consumer of textiles and manufactured products of Britain. They told the great mercantile houses that they could bring coal by rail to Calcutta from the mines of West Bengal and become even wealthier. They put together a powerful coalition in Parliament, and together they exerted great pressure on the British government. They succeeded in the end, getting hugely favourable contracts that allowed them to raise funds in Britain to build and manage their railway operations in India—much of it guaranteed by the government against any risk of loss. There could not have been a better deal.

The East Indian Railway Company was one of the first to get going. It built and operated a line running a few dozen miles north of Calcutta along the Hooghly river. Later, it extended it to the coalmines, 100 miles north-west of Calcutta, and subsequently to the well-populated and fertile Ganges valley. About the same time, the Great Indian Peninsula Railway Company constructed a second line running north from Bombay for thirty-five miles to Kalyan, which it expanded later over the Western Ghats into the rich cotton fields of the Deccan. Many lines followed thereafter. The cost of construction was high, as our authors point out, partly because the companies had a guaranteed return of cost plus five per cent. They had little incentive to economize, and they built carelessly and lavishly. When the work was defective, they simply rebuilt. They erected stations in a grand style and provided luxury coaches for upper-class passengers.

Thus was one of the world's greatest railway systems built. It was the largest single injection of British capital into India's economy, and the network went on to become the third largest in the world. At Independence, in 1947, it was more than 50,000 miles long, employing more than a million men, with 9000 locomotives, 225,000 freight cars, and more than 16,000 passenger coaches.

As we noted, the railways had a profound effect on millions of lives as people began to move and merchants began to send their goods to distant parts of the country. New towns came up along the railway lines. However, there was also a downside. Artisans in villages and towns began to lose their living because they could not compete with British-manufactured goods that began to arrive rapidly. Earlier, the peasants had stored their surplus grains in the good years. Now the railways began to carry food and commercial crops to the ports for export. Reserves were thus depleted, and in the devastating famine years of the 1870s and 1890s, there was no stored surplus to fall back on. It would have needed a more benign and far-thinking government to prevent the downside.

~

The railways were born of the industrial revolution. The authors of this book begin with a famous quote from Karl Marx, who predicted that railways would create an industrial revolution in India and transform the country. They did not. But how did British capital, which also built railways in America, bring about an industrial revolution there? I learned at university that exchange is natural to human beings, and if you create the conditions for exchange—like infrastructure, such as the railways—economic activity will arise spontaneously. One should have expected entrepreneurs to respond vigorously in an industrial age, creating small and big industries in the vicinity of the railways; an industrial revolution should have been the result.

This remains one of the intriguing questions of history. Indeed, by the First World War, some thought India was ready to take off. Our authors inform us that India had 28,000 miles of rail track by 1905, making it the third largest railway network in the world. India also had the world's largest jute manufacturing industry, the fourth largest cotton textile industry, the largest canal system, and 2.5 per cent of world trade. It also had a merchant class hungry to become industrialists.

Indeed, after World War I, industrialization did accelerate. G.D. Birla, Kasturbhai Lalbhai and other businessmen made huge trading profits during World War I and reinvested them in setting up industries. Between 1913 and 1938, Indian manufacturing output grew 5.6 per cent a year, well ahead of the world average of 3.3 per cent. By 1947, industry's share of national output doubled to 7.5 per cent from 3.4 per cent. Yet, it was not enough to transform India's agricultural society broadly. Modern industry, alas, employed only 2.5 million people out of a population of 350 million. The authors of this volume point out that the railway network had neglected freight, and also that its construction had bypassed significant geographical parts of the country. Moreover, India's agriculture remained stagnant. You cannot have an industrial revolution without an agricultural surplus or the means to feed a rapidly growing urban population.

In the end, the spread effects of this great investment were limited. By contrast, Japan's railways, built at the same time, delivered more positive results. The Japanese had economized with their limited capital and had built a more geographically intensive network. The Indian railway network, although huge in absolute terms, was comparatively small, in both per-capita and per-square mile terms. In 1937, India had twenty-six miles of railway lines per 1000 square miles of land, when the US had 80 and Germany 253. This partially explains why the railways did not engender an industrial revolution in India. Sadly, the massive construction of the railways was not enough to modernize the Indian economy. India alone, among the great railway countries, remained relatively un-industrialized. In the other railway powers—the United States, Russia and Germany—the railway had been a dynamo of the industrial revolution. It had no such effect in India. Nevertheless, it is a powerful British legacy in a landscape of backwardness. Without the railways, India would have been even less industrialized.

Indian nationalists have blamed the British Raj for this failure. Marx believed that capital exploits, and Indian nationalists jumped on this bandwagon to argue that British capital was 'exploitive'. I disagree. Anyone who wanted India to become modern, prosperous and middle class should have wanted loads of investment. In fact, Britain did not 'exploit' India enough. Had it made the enormous investments in India that it did in the Americas, India would have become prosperous and a much bigger market for British goods. A richer India would have been even a better customer and a better supplier. An impoverished India was not in Britain's economic interest.

Our nationalists have failed to comprehend that capital is a progressive force, however exploitative it may appear. Marx understood this. He knew that capitalism is the only efficient way to accumulate capital, make investments, raise output, and increase productivity. Even today, many Indians, with their phobia of multinationals, have not learned this lesson. Even the nationalists, who understood that foreign investment is positive, felt there was a British conspiracy to deliberately under-invest in India, or to sabotage Indian business interests.

Again, I disagree. Businessmen invest whenever and wherever profit is to be made, and their decisions have little to do with nationalism. British business was not a homogeneous force. The textile mills owned by Indians in the nineteenth century were built with the credit, technical assistance and machines from the British textile machinery makers, even when these mills were a competitive threat to the Manchester mills. Burn and Co., a full-blooded European company, did not hesitate to make inland river steam vessels in India when they found it cheaper than importing them from Britain. Companies generally look to their bottom line and do not fly the flag of their parent countries.

~

Today, Indian Railways are the Indian government in miniature—good in quantity but poor in quality. Every day they weave a nation together. In 2015–16, they sold 8.6 billion tickets, which translates into roughly seven journeys per person per year. A nation is on the move, thanks in part to the railways. The poorest Indian is mobile because railway tickets are cheaper than almost anywhere in the world. This is the good news!

The bad news is that the Indian Railways are inefficient, hopelessly over-manned, utterly politicized, sometimes corrupt, and provide shoddy, callous service. No one dreams of transporting goods by rail, not only because tariffs are uncompetitively high (since freight subsidizes passenger fares) but also because there are constant delays as goods trains are not timetabled. As a result, even coal, petrol and diesel are inefficiently transported by road. This bias against freight is, of course, a historical one, as the authors of this volume point out.

One sometimes feels that the purpose of Indian Railways is not to serve customers but to tend to the comforts of the 1.3 million employees who have jobs for life. Employees account for 50 per cent of railway costs in India, and reflect seven times more manpower per kilometre than in developed railway countries. Friends and families of railway employees occupy, on average, 40 out of 100 berths in the two-tier (AC) sleeper class, and get priority in bookings. Because of rising payroll costs, expenses on repairs and maintenance have been steadily declining, while employee negligence (called 'human error') is the main cause of accidents. The safety record of the railways is poor. When the Rajdhani train derailed on the Tundla-Kanpur section in January 1992, the chief area manager of Kanpur was transferred not for safety reasons, but because he was aiding injured passengers and not looking after the visiting chairman of the Railway Board.

To become an efficient, contemporary, high-performing institution, the railways have to take many steps, and these have been clearly articulated over the years by numerous committees, including the one headed by one of the authors of this book. The starting point is to recognize that monopolies are bad—and Indian Railways remains one of the last railway monopolies in the world. In the past three decades, country after country has broken the monopoly of its state-owned railway. The results of these efforts have been spectacular: services have improved, customers are empowered and happier, the balance sheets of the railway companies are stronger, and the state no longer carries the financial burden of subsidy. This experience has disproved the old myth that railways are a natural monopoly. If one separated the company that manages the rail track and infrastructure from the one that runs the trains, the customer would have the choice of a second Shatabdi, run by a competitor, and the service and quality on the original Shatabdi would also improve.

This anecdotal history of Indian Railways by Debroy and others has wisely confined itself to the story up to the time of Independence. It touches upon many other issues. One of these is the question of public versus private management of infrastructure. Many of the railways in India were built privately and later taken over. Another question is that of infrastructure financing. The government got embroiled in the notorious problem of guaranteeing a fixed return on investment to private entrepreneurs. Its purpose was to mitigate the risk associated with an uncertain technology in an uncertain part of the world. A third question is whether the railways, in fact, made money. The authors tell us that the cumulative losses of the railways until 1884 exceeded half a million pounds. The broader question is: should infrastructure make money? It seems reasonable to expect that users ought to pay enough so that the institution, whether public or private, does not lose money.

These are the sort of issues that engage our authors in Penguin's unique multi-volume series, The Story of Indian Business. This series, as a whole, attempts to mine great ideas in business and economics that have shaped commerce in the bazaars and on the high seas of the Indian Ocean. Leading contemporary scholars and writers examine historical texts, inscriptions and records, and interpret them in a lively, sharp and authoritative manner for the intelligent reader who may have no prior background in the field. Each slender volume offers an enduring perspective on business enterprise of the past. It seeks to entertain and edify, avoiding the pitfall of simplistically cataloguing a set of lessons for today. The value of the exercise is to promote a longer-term sensibility in the reader for an understanding of the material bases of the present human condition and to think realistically about our economic future. Taken together, our series celebrates the ideal captured by the ancient Indian goal of life called *artha*.

The series began with Tom Trautmann's reinterpretation for our times of the renowned treatise on the science of wealth, *Arthashastra*, which was authored almost 2000 years ago and is considered the world's first manual on political economy. Kanakalatha Mukund took us south in the next volume, *The World of the Tamil Merchant*, to a beguiling trading world when one of the ports of south India was receiving at least one ship from Rome every day. Mukund has reconstructed this world by drawing on the epics, *Silappadikaram*, *Manimekalai* and other historical materials relating to the Chola empire. Next, we jumped a few centuries to Tirthankar Roy's account of the East India Company, which taught us, among other things, how much the modern multinational corporation is a child of the company that ruled India and is mostly reviled today.

Our fourth volume hopped to the late eighteenth century, to the time of decline of the port of Surat and the rise of Bombay. In it, Lakshmi Subramanian recounted vividly the ups and downs of the adventurous lives of three merchants in *Three Merchants of Bombay: Trawadi Arjunji Nathji, Jamsetjee Jeejeebhoy and Premchand Roychand*. Arshia Sattar returned to India's classical past to narrate in the fifth volume some charming merchant adventures in *The Mouse Merchant* and other tales based on the *Kathasaritsagara*, *Panchatantra* and other sources. In the next volume, Tom Timberg's *Marwaris* examined the bold, risk-taking world of India's most famous business community. It quickly became a popular best-seller. In the seventh volume, Scott Levi took us back to the early modern period and recounted the saga of the Punjabi Khatri traders from Multan, who took caravans on the 'Silk Road' across the Himalayas to Central Asia and beyond to Russia from 1500 to 1850. After that, Chhaya Goswami and Jaithirth Rao dove deep into the Indian Ocean of the eighteenth century to recount the tales of Gujarati merchants from Kachchh in the trade triangle of Mandvi, Muscat and Zanzibar. In the ninth volume, Omkar Goswami described a new way of organizing business—the managing agency—which arose in India with the decline of the East India Company and was popular among both the English and Indians for a century and a half.

Professor Donald Davis will raise contemporary issues in a forthcoming book about the dharma of business in an engaging study of pre-modern commercial law based on medieval commentaries on the *Dharmasastras*. We have plans for a book on trade tales from Mughal India, and for another on the Indian Ocean. Three other business communities—the Chettiars, the Parsis, and the Jains— will be featured in future volumes. Finally, Medha Kudaisiya will round off the series, recording a story of betrayal in the historic 'Bombay Plan' on the future shape of independent India's economy, drawn by eminent industrialists in 1944–45.

Gurcharan Das

PREFACE

In 2014, the Railway Board and the ministry of railways set up a committee that went by the rather formidable title of 'High Powered Committee for Mobilization of Resources for Major Railway Projects and Restructuring of Railway Ministry and Railway Board'. The committee's final report was submitted in June 2015. But that is beside the point. This book has nothing to do with that Committee or its report. After all, that Committee was about solving the current problems at Indian Railways.

However, that committee and its mandate got three very different individuals working together. Bibek Debroy was chairman of the committee, and Sanjay Chadha the secretary. And it was Vidya Krishnamurthi who, then a 'Young Professional' at Niti Aayog—Niti Aayog is the successor to the former Planning Commission, established in January 2015, with a mandate somewhat different from that of the former Planning Commission—helped draft the committee's report. As work progressed, we realized that we were not just interested in Indian Railways as it currently existed, but were also equally interested in the Indian Railways of yesterday. We were curious about its historical evolution and had accumulated an inventory of facts and trivia about it.

That committee also brought a fourth individual into the picture. Gurcharan Das, also a member of the committee, happened to be the general editor for this Penguin (India) series. He asked us to put together an anecdotal history of Indian Railways. This book is the result of that suggestion. It is a great chronicle of voices and vignettes, trains and tracks. Gurcharan Das also gave us valuable comments on the draft manuscript, and the final product is a better book for that.

Why should there be another book on the railways in India? Aren't there plenty floating around—Nalinaksha Sanyal's *Development of Indian Railways* (University of Calcutta, 1930), Ian J. Kerr's *Building the Railways of the Raj, 1850–1900* (Oxford University Press, 1995), Laura Bear's *Lines of the Nation: Indian Railway Workers, Bureaucracy, and the Intimate Historical Shelf* (Columbia University Press, 2007), Marian Aguiar's *Tracking Modernity: India's Railway and the Culture of Mobility* (University of Minnesota Press, 2011)? There are many more: there is a long bibliography in a book by Ian Kerr and John Hurd; and more books and dissertations are added to this list every year. But most of the books on these lists are based on academic work. No matter how good the quality of writing, they tend to be dry and boring, unattractive to the general reader. At the other end of the spectrum there are coffee table-type books, rich in photographs and light in text, typically brought out when Indian Railways celebrated 150 years, or when its individual zones celebrated their centenaries. We wanted to do a cross between the two types, the academic and the coffee table. You could say that we have done a Rajendra Aklekar (*Halt Station India—The Dramatic Tale of the Nation's First Rail-lines*, Rupa Publications, 2014) for the entire span of India's railway history, and without any geographical biases. Whether this has worked, only the reader can judge.

We have liberally used information from the IRFCA (Indian Railways Fan Club Association) website. But in the process, we also believe we unearthed a few nuggets of our own, not reported elsewhere.

History implies a timeline, and that needs to be pinned down too. The conventional date for the start of Indian Railways is 1853, though the seeds were sown in the 1830s. That's when we start our narrative, which we end with India's Independence. The story of what happened to the railways after Independence is a separate one. Although themes go backwards and forwards and cannot always be neatly segregated into chronological timelines, our story sticks to a chronological template; accordingly, the chapters of this book are determined by chronology and not theme.

Much of the romance associated with Indian Railways is identified with the initial years and with the era of steam. That bias has crept into our account too, and we have deliberately not sought to change it.

The table below should help the reader keep track of the timeline that runs through this book. We hope references to this table will help the reader as they advance through the book.

Timeline of establishment of railway companies and railway lines in India

Timeline	Railway Companies	Railway Lines
1845	East Indian Railway Company (EIRC)	
1851		Experimental line from Calcutta to Rajmahal
1854		First passenger train in eastern India—Howrah to Hooghly
1855		Experimental line up to Raneegunje
1862		Jamalpur Locomotive Workshop established
1871		Main line on Calcutta–Delhi route completed
1880		EIR taken over by state (construction and operation by company) Bengal Nagpur Railway (BNR) formed
1892		Assam Bengal Railway formed

Timeline	Railway Companies	Railway Lines
1849	Great Indian Peninsula Railway (GIPR)	
1853		First passenger train from Boree Bunder to Tannah (Bombay to Thane)
1858		Khandala to Poona traffic opened
1867		Bombay to Calcutta—Thull Ghat connected to Bhusawal, two bifurcations 1) Amravati to Nagpore 2) Jabalpur to Allahabad, connected with Allahabad to the Jabalpur branch line of EIR
1870		Howrah–Allahabad–Bombay line opened
1853	Madras Railway Company	For railway line Madras–Beypore–Madras
1856		Royapuram–Arcot: This line helped to connect Madras with Bangalore and Bombay

Timeline	Railway Companies	Railway Lines
1864		Madras–Beypore and Bangalore Cantonment line opened
1871	Merged with Southern Mahratta Railway and renamed in 1908	Extension up to Raichur linked with GIPR (from Kalyan to Raichur)
1908	Madras and Southern Mahratta Railway formed	
1908		Nilgiri Mountain Railway linking Mettupalayam and Coonoor
1855	Sindh Railway Company	
1861		Karachi to Kotri
1870		Amalgamated into Scinde, Punjab & Delhi Railways Company
1886		Further amalgamated with state-owned railways to create North Western State Railway and Sind, Delhi, Punjab Railway Company

Timeline	Railway Companies	Railway Lines
1889		Karachi–Keamari line
1897		Keamari–Kotri line
1855	Bombay, Baroda and Central Railway Company (BB&CI)	Surat to Bombay
1861		Bombay connected to Baroda
1863		Line to Ahmedabad
1871		Line to Viramgaon
1857	Great Southern of India Railway Company	
1861		Line from Negapatnam to Tiruvallur to Tanjore
1862		Line extended to Trichinopoly
1866		Line from Trichinopoly to Karur
1867		Line from Karur to Kodumudi
1868		Line from Kodumudi to Erode
1869	Carnatic Railway	

Timeline	Railway Companies	Railway Lines
1874	Great Southern of India Railway & Carnatic Railway merged Now called South Indian Railway (SIR)	
1879	Pondicherry Railway company (under supervision of SIR)	
		Villupuram to Gingee branch Pondicherry to Villupuram
1857	Eastern Bengal Railway Company	
1879–1881		New Jalpaiguri to Darjeeling

Timeline	Railway Companies	Railway Lines
1862	Indian Branch Railway Company (IBRC)	
1863		Azimganj to Nalhati
1867	Government takes over, renaming it Nalhati State	Metre gauge—Kanpur to Lucknow branch line
1872	Railway (branch line)	
1872	Main line renamed Oudh and Rohilkhand Railway Company	Lucknow to Sandila to Hardoi
1873		Extension of line to Bareilly
1874		Lucknow to Varanasi—linked with EIR's branch line of Mogul Sarai
1886		Main line, Moradabad to Sahranpur

Timeline	Railway Companies	Railway Lines
1870	Emergence of Native State Railways	
1878	Nagpur Chhattisgarh Railway (NCR)	Nagpur to Rajnandgaon via Tumsar-Gondia and Dongargarh
1888	NCR purchased by Bengal Nagpur Railway from GIPR	
1891		Nagpur to Asansol
1900	GIPR's Nagpur branch connected with BNR	Line connected to Howrah
1880	Assam Railways and Trading Company (AR&TC)	Line from Dibrugarh to Sadiya and branch line from Makum to Talup

Timeline	Railway Companies	Railway Lines
1882	Southern Mahratta Railway	
1884		Bellary to Hospet
1887		Londa to Portuguese Goa
1890		Railway line along the coast, Marmagoa to Beswada
1907	Merged with Madras Railway, renamed Southern and Maratha Railway	
1883	Rohilkhand Kumaun Railway	Lines from Kumaun in Uttarakhand to western Uttar Pradesh
1891		Lucknow to Bareilly
1883	Jorhat Provincial Railway (JPR)	Jorhat–Mariani section of Tinsukia Division Mariani–Furkating

Timeline	Railway Companies	Railway Lines
1885	Indian Midland Railway Company	
1889		Lines from Jhansi to Gwalior, Kanpur, Manikpur and Bhopal
1892	Assam Bengal Railways	
1895		Chittagong–Comilla (Bangladesh) branch line to Guwahati
1896–98		Comilla–Akhaura–Kalaura–Badarpur
1898	Delhi–Ambala–Kalka Railway Company	Kalka–Shimla railway
1901	Neral–Matheran Light Railway Built by Indian businessman Adamjee Peerbhoy	

Timeline	Railway Companies	Railway Lines
1906	Flying Ranee	Bombay–Surat Suspended in 1914 and reintroduced in 1937 Suspended during World War II
1912	Punjab Limited (GIPR)	Bombay–Peshawar
1926	Imperial Mail (GIPR)	Bombay–Calcutta
1930		Deccan Queen—Bombay to Poona

I

THE 1830S: INCEPTION

'The railway-system will therefore become, in India, truly the forerunner of modern industry.' Many will be familiar with this quotation from Karl Marx. They may not necessarily remember where Marx wrote this and when. His observation is from a piece titled 'The Future Results of British Rule in India'.[1] A more complete extract is the following:

> The millocracy have discovered that the transformation of India into a reproductive country has become of vital importance to them, and that, to that end, it is necessary, above all, to gift her with means of irrigation and of internal communication. They intend now drawing a net of railroads over

---

[1] *Marx and Engels Collected Works*, Vol. 12, Lawrence & Wishart, 1979.

India . . . I know that the English millocracy intend
to endow India with railways with the exclusive
view of extracting at diminished expenses the cotton
and other raw materials for their manufactures.
But when you have once introduced machinery
into the locomotion of a country, which possesses
iron and coals, you are unable to withhold it
from its fabrication. You cannot maintain a net
of railways over an immense country without
introducing all those industrial processes necessary
to meet the immediate and current wants of railway
locomotion, and out of which there must grow
the application of machinery to those branches of
industry not immediately connected with railways.
The railway-system will therefore become, in India,
truly the forerunner of modern industry. This is
the more certain as the Hindoos are allowed by
British authorities themselves to possess particular
aptitude for accommodating themselves to entirely
new labor, and acquiring the requisite knowledge of
machinery. Ample proof of this fact is afforded by
the capacities and expertness of the native engineers
in the Calcutta mint, where they have been for years
employed in working the steam machinery, by the
natives attached to the several steam engines in the
Burdwan coal districts, and by other instances.

When did Karl Marx write this piece? He wrote it on
22 July 1853, though it was first published on 8 August
1853. 1853 is important because that's the official

date—16 April, to be precise—for the start of the railways in India, and Marx must have known about this.

(Thus, in the centennial year in 1953, a postage stamp was issued to celebrate the occasion.)

Railway development was relatively new in 1853—not just in India, but everywhere in the world. Therefore, expectations about what the railways would do for economic development, industrial progress and productivity were no more than, well, expectations. With the benefit of hindsight, we now know that, compared with what happened in many other countries in the world, India's railway development didn't quite bring those benefits—the benefits that economists refer to as 'positive externalities'.

'Conceptually, there is a strong case for channelling resources to transport infrastructure in India given the widely known spillover effects of transport networks to link markets, reduce a variety of costs, boost agglomeration economies, and improve the competitiveness of the economy, especially manufacturing which tends to be logistics-intensive.' This is a quotation not from 1853, but from the government of India's 2014–15 Economic Survey.[2] If this was being said in February 2015, presumably, the expectations of 1853 had fallen somewhat short. There were two reasons for this, both rather sweeping statements. First, freight was neglected, and the emphasis was on passengers. Second, major

---

[2] *Economic Survey, 2014–15, Volume I*, Department of Economic Affairs, Ministry of Finance, February 2015.

geographical parts of the country were bypassed in the process of railway development.

Courtesy IRFCA

In 1953, the centennial year of Indian Railways, India issued a postage stamp to celebrate the occasion. But the date 1853 is both right and wrong; the postage stamp is both right and wrong. At 3.35 p.m., on 16 April 1853, flagged off with a twenty-one-gun salute, a train with fourteen railway carriages and 400 guests left Bori Bunder for Thane (then Tannah). With three steam locomotives (Sindh, Sultan and Sahib) it took one hour and fifteen minutes to make the journey. Bori Bunder station is no longer used. A non-stop EMU (electric multiple unit) train from Chhatrapati Shivaji Terminus to Thane still takes fifty-seven minutes! The Bori Bunder–Tannah journey of 16 April 1853 was the first commercial passenger service, but not the first train in the country. Karl Marx clearly knew this, since he talked about steam engines in the Burdwan coal districts. But IR (Indian Railways) decided to celebrate its centenary year in 1953. It must be placed on record that no photograph exists of the 1853 journey. And the reader should keep in mind that any photograph or postage stamp purportedly showing that train should have pictured three engines, not one. No one seems to know what happened to the locomotives Sahib and Sultan. They just vanished. Sindh was luckier. The locomotive was last seen on a plinth at what used to be the Byculla office of GIPR (Great Indian Peninsula Railway). Sindh was brought to Delhi by Indian Railways later, but no one knows what happened to Sindh thereafter.

The 1953 fare from Bombay to Thane was Rs 2 and 10 annas for first class travel, Re 1 and 1 anna for a second class ticket, and 5 annas and 3 pice for the third class. However, this was for the subsequent journeys, and not for that first train ride in April 1853. Since all 400 passengers were invited VIPs, including Lady Falkland, wife of the governor of Bombay, they probably paid nothing. An apocryphal story tells us that the governor, Lord Falkland, didn't think the railway line was a terribly good idea, and wasn't part of the entourage.

If quiz book facts need to be amended a bit about the first train in India, one should mention 1837 and Chintadripet. The Madras Presidency of the British owed its origins to Madraspatnam, a fisherman's village. There were other villages in Madras Presidency, and one of these was Chintadripet, or Chinna Thari Pettai, to use the original name. The grey marking at the centre of the map shows us

where Chintadripet lay.[3] Chintadripet means a 'village of
small looms'. This village was established in 1735, when the
governor of Fort St George was George Morton Pitt. One
of the merchants of the city possessed a garden where the
River Cooum winds past Periampet. A village for spinners,
weavers, washermen, painters and temple attendants was
established in that large garden. This became Chintadripet.
A railway outfit called Red Hill Railroad (RHR) is associated
with the name of Chintadripet. There is occasional, cursory
mention of this in many written records, before even
references to Bori Bunder–Thane[4] in any records.

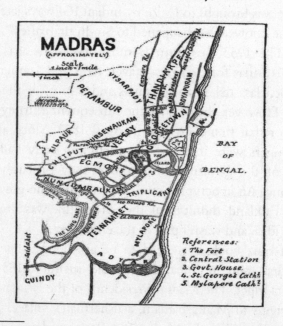

---

[3] *The Story of Madras*, Glyn Barlow, Oxford University Press, 1921.
[4] See, *Indian Railways: Glorious 150 years*, R.R. Bhandari, Ministry
of Information and Broadcasting, Government of India, 2005.

The Red Hill Railroad was built in 1836, two decades before the Bori Bunder–Thane railway. The best account of this relatively neglected railway line is in a piece written by Simon Darvill,[5] from which we learn the following. First, it wasn't quite an experimental line. There was probably an initial three-mile-long line from Red Hills— to the north of Madras City, which gets its name from the red hills there—to the stone quarries around Little Mount—a small hillock in Chennai, along the banks of the River Adyar—but this eventually merged with RHR's permanent line. Second, it was built to carry granite for road-building work, leading to an estimated annual savings of Rs 28,000 on a Rs 60,000 budget for building roads in the Presidency. It was a freight railway, but passengers also travelled on it. Third, though it was planned for animals to pull the train, two or three steam locomotives (one of which was built by the Madras Corps of Engineers) were also used. Fourth, the rolling stock possibly consisted of road-carts on railway wheels. Fifth, the rails were produced in Parangipettai (Cuddalore district). Sixth, the railway cost Rs 50,000 crore to build.

More than one newspaper report on the railway is available on the IRFCA website. From the *Madras Gazette* of 4 May 1836:

A small piece of railway has been laid down near the Chintadripet Bridge to show how little

---

[5] 'India's First Railways', Simon Darvill, 2011, http://www.irfca. org/docs/history/india-first-railways.html

labour is required on a road of this description, a cart is placed upon the rails, loaded with stones, which is easily moved up a slightly inclined plane by one hand, from whence it returns by its own weight to the place from which it was first propelled . . . which is worth the inspection of the good people of Madras who have not visited England since railways have been common.

And from the *Conservative* of 6 May 1836:

We have reason to know that the state of the railway question, as far as the Government are concerned, is as follows:- The attention of the Government was attracted to the large and unproductive expenditure upon the public roads of this presidency, and the board of revenue were, in consequence, desired to report whether a more economical and efficient system could not be introduced, and whether it might not be advisable in some instances to substitute railroads for common roads. The board referred the subject to Capt. Cotton, who after inspection of the localities, expressed confident opinion, that by laying rails to the Red Hills, and to the Stone Quarries at the Little Mount, a saving of nearly one half, or about Rs 28,000 out of annual expenditure of about Rs 60,000 might be affected

in the conveyance of materials alone for the
presidency roads, besides yielding a revenue by the
conveyance of private trade. He recommended,
therefore, that immediate measures should be
taken for surveying the lines and framing detailed
estimates. His proposal was approved, and orders
issued accordingly, and also for laying down
the experimental railway at Chintadripet, as an
experiment.

The *Asiatic Journal* of August 1837 reported:

The temporary Red Hills Railroad has already
been completed though for a time rendered
useless in consequence of a portion of the
embankment of the canal having given way where
the railroad joins on it, requiring in consequence
the former to be carried on somewhat farther.
The temporary railroad has cost the Government
50,000 rupees. It extends from the Red Hills to the
canal, a distance of about three miles and a half,
and is qualified only to bear a weight of about a
ton and a half. To be made a permanent structure
that is by exchanging the wooden for iron-stone
or laterite supports it will cost Rs 14 or 15 lakhs
more.

The Red Hill Railway was closed in 1845. On the closure,
Simon Darvill wrote,

It is unknown how long the RHR was in use for. In an extensive article in *The Foreign Quarterly Review*, written in May 1845, about the prospect of building a railway system in India, a footnote concerning the RHRR stated that, 'The Red Hill Railway was dependent on a canal and as that occasionally dried up, the railroad could not possibly answer (*sic*); for when there was no water to float the barges, the trains which brought down granite to fill them could not of course be needed.' . . . From the fact that the railway is referred to in the past tense, it can be inferred that it had closed prior to the article being written. It is known from the paper about the locomotives[6] that experiments ceased abruptly after the second test as Capt. Cotton had become ill and went to Tasmania on sick leave. It would be a good supposition that the railway's decline came after Cotton left Madras as he was the driving force behind the railway; it was certainly the reason for the cessation of experiments with locomotives. Whatever the reason, it was the end of railways and locomotive traction in India for the time being.

The Capt. Cotton in question is Arthur Thomas Cotton (1803–1899), identified more with the construction of irrigation and navigational canals, especially in Andhra Pradesh and Tamil Nadu. Cotton is the one who proposed

---

[6] The paper was written by Captain J.T. Smith of the Corps of Engineers, Madras Presidency.

that experimental line in Chintadripet. Those cost figures were also his estimates. With Arthur Cotton away in Tasmania, interest in the railway also declined, temporarily. Arthur Cotton fell ill more than once, resulting in his travelling to Tasmania thrice, between 1838 and 1843. The choice of Tasmania had to do with the East India Company's sick leave rules.[7] The word 'furlough' means leave of absence. The East India Company had furlough rules. These 1796 rules were liberalized in 1854, and again in 1868. A letter of complaint, printed in the *Spectator* on 11 September 1852, explains the problem with the 1796 furlough rules:[8]

> By the present furlough regulations, an officer is entitled after ten years' actual service in India to a furlough of three years, on very reduced allowances. He forfeits any appointment he may hold by going to England, and the period of his furlough is deducted from the term of service which entitles him to a retiring pension. After he has once taken his furlough, there is no second open to him. By a strange anomaly, he is permitted to take his furlough to New South Wales, or any place East of the Cape of Good Hope, without incurring any of these penalties except the last. His allowances are not reduced, or in

---

[7] 'Arthur Cotton and Irrigation in Tasmania, 1839–43,' G. Blackburn, *Papers and Proceedings of the Royal Society of Tasmania*, No. 119, 1985.

[8] http://archive.spectator.co.uk/article/11th-september-1852/12/furlough-regulations-of-the-indian-army

a very much slighter degree; he does not forfeit his appointment if he holds one; and the time that he is absent 'counts for service'. The regulations are, in fact, as you may perceive, a very high protective duty on the East Indies and Oriental residence.

This applied to sick leave too. As a result, when he fell ill, Arthur Cotton preferred to go to Tasmania and not to London. Naturally, 'furlough' was not valid in India. But for the furlough rules, Cotton might not have gone to Tasmania and got interested in irrigation, and RHR might have survived.

Having gone to Tasmania, Cotton developed an interest in irrigation while there. In any irrigation/canals-versus-railways debate, Arthur Cotton was on the irrigation/canals side of the debate, as evidenced by his 1854 monograph:[9]

If this be all that the most perfect railways can do for India, and if there were no other means by which something could be accomplished, our case would be hopeless indeed. If India is to advance in anything, it must have cheap transit, really cheap transit, at one-tenth or one-twentieth of the present rates. In planning the great railways, the real points to be attended to have been entirely lost sight of;

[9] *Public Works in India, Their Importance; With Suggestions for their Extension and Improvement*, Richardson Brothers, London, 1854, https://archive.org/stream/publicworksinin01cottgoog#page/n6/mode/2up

and this first one especially. When the projectors talk of charging 1d. to 3d. per ton per mile, they do not consider the fact, that a good common road will carry at 1½d.; and that the imperfect unimproved natural water transit where it exists, costs only ½d.[10]

Despite Cotton's preference for waterways and irrigation works (his name is associated with the Dowleswaram Barrage on the Godavari and the Cotton Museum in Rajamundry), it must be recalled that he not only thought up the Chintadripet railway line, temporary though it was, but also had in mind, as early as in 1836, a railway line connecting Madras with Bombay via a route of about 862 miles through Wallajahnagore, Arcot, Nellore, Bangalore, Bellary and Poona.

However, though the 1830s marked the inception of the railways in India, the 1840s made for marking time and debating.

---

[10] *Ibid.*

2

THE 1840S: DISCOURSE, DEBATE AND MARKING TIME

The 1840s were a decade of marking time, discourse and debate. Though trains would not run till the 1850s, two major railway companies were formed in the 1840s—the East India Railway Company (EICR) in 1845 and the Great Indian Peninsular Railway (GIPR) in 1849. The Madras Railway Company (MRC) was formed a little later, in 1853. The debates happened through official reports and correspondence, surveys and newspaper articles. They involved both the British and Indians. There was a special interest in Bombay and Calcutta. In Britain, the 1840s have been described as an era of railway mania, when a bubble had been created through overinvestments in stocks of relatively unregulated railway companies.[11] This

---

[11] See, for example, 'Collective hallucinations and inefficient markets', Andrew Odlyzko, University of Minnesota, 2010,

had its spillover effects in India too: 'The Report[12] can be placed in the general background of the English railway mania of 1844–47, which was transplanted from the metropolis of London to both Europe and the Empire by investors, contractors and promoters. The mania invaded India in the early 1840s, infiltrating Bombay and Calcutta, where the railway question was busily discussed and acted upon during this period.'[13]

The prime supporters of railway development were Rowland Macdonald Stephenson (1808–95) and Lord Dalhousie. Stephenson had much more than Calcutta or India on his mind. He had railway plans for China too, linking Calcutta, Peking and Hong Kong, and visited Hong Kong in 1859 to find support for this idea.[14] In 1844, John Chapman (1801–54) prepared the first proposal for the GIPR, and this received the support of Stephenson too. As for Stephenson himself, he submitted his first private proposal to the East India Company in 1841. But this proposal was dismissed as a 'wild idea'.[15] Undeterred, he eventually—after dabbling in journalism for a while—left for Calcutta in 1843, to try and persuade government of

---

http://www.dtc.umn.edu/~odlyzko/doc/hallucinations.pdf

[12] The 1844 Rowland Macdonald Stephenson Report, cited below.

[13] 'The Colonial Context of the Bengal Renaissance: A Note on Early Railway-Thinking in Bengal,' Dipesh Chakrabarty, in, Roopa Srinivasan, Manish Tiwari and Sandeep Silas edited, *Our Indian Railway, Themes in India's Railway History*, Foundation Books, 2006.

[14] See, *Privatized Infrastructure: The Role of Government,* Adrian J. Smith, Thomas Telford, 1999.

[15] http://www.irfca.org/articles/eminent-railwaymen.html

India officials to consider his proposal. In Calcutta, he wrote a piece in the *Englishman* in 1844, advocating railways for India. There were six main railway lines in his proposed structure: (1) from Calcutta to Mirzapur/Delhi through the coalfields and with an extension to Firozpur; (2) from Bombay, joining the first line at Mirzapur; (3) from Bombay to Hyderabad, leading on to Calcutta; (4) from Hyderabad to Madras; (5) a line from Madras to Bangalore, Mysore and Calicut; and (6) a line from Madras to the southernmost tip of the country, via Arcot, Tiruchirapally and Tirunelveli.[16] The layout was determined either by military considerations or by the need to facilitate export of raw materials and import of finished goods.

> The first consideration is as a military measure for the better security with less outlay, of the entire territory, the second is in a commercial point of view, in which the chief object is to provide the means of conveyance from the interior to the nearest shipping ports of the rich and varied productions of the country, and to transmit back manufactured goods of Great Britain, salt, etc. in exchange.[17]

The famous 1844/45 report followed.[18] The EICR was formally constituted in 1845, and Stephenson became the

---

[16] *Eminent Railwaymen of Yesteryears*, R.R. Bhandari, 2008, http://www.irfca.org/articles/eminent-railwaymen.html

[17] Extracted in the 1845 Report, cited below.

[18] *Report Upon the Practicality and Advantages of the Introduction of Railways into British India*, R. Macdonald Stephenson, Kelly

first agent and chief engineer. Stephenson actually thought of a railway line connecting London and Calcutta, with two breaks—one at the English Channel and the other at the Dardanelles. In 1850, he wrote to Viscount Palmerston,[19]

> The European lines already completed are from the port on the British channel to Vienna, the distance about 1000 miles which will be hereafter reduced to about 700 miles. The Austrian extension to the frontier will be 300 miles. The distance on either side of Istanbul will be through European Turkey 500 miles and through Asiatic Turkey 1300 miles, in all 2800 miles from the channel port to the port on the Persian Gulf. This would constitute the first step, the passage to Bombay 1600 miles, being made by steamer and thence by railway to Calcutta and the interiors of India. The second step embraces the extension from the port on the Persian Gulf through Persia 550 miles and through Baluchistan 550 miles to the Indus, a distance of 1100 miles. The connection with the North West Province and southward with the Narmada Valley would complete the chain of communication by the East

& Company, 1845, https://ia601409.us.archive.org/27/items/reportuponpract00stepgoog/reportuponpract00stepgoog.pdf. This carried extracts from the 1844 *Englishman* article and may well explain a minor inconsistency. The Report is often dated to 1844. However, it was actually published in 1845, though it carried extracts from the 1844 article.

[19] Bhandari, *op. cit.*

Indian, and Indian Peninsular lines with Calcutta and Bombay. The third step which will connect the East Indian trunk line through the Nepalese range of the Himalayas with the river Tsangpo will open up to the entire trade with China and the Eastern seas by means of the river Yangtze-kiang and Mekong.

At that time, nothing much could be done with this idea, not even when it was raised with Lord Dalhousie in 1856. It was premature, and Lord Dalhousie minuted,

Mr. Ronald Stephenson waited upon me some days ago, for the purpose of submitting a plan which he had projected for uniting Europe with India by a line of Railway communication continued through Asiatic Turkey. It has been at my suggestion that the plan is not laid before the Government of India.... The project consists of a proposal for continuing the European Railways, already completed (I am informed) as far as Belgrade and about to be constructed from Belgrade to Istanbul by a line of rail and from Istanbul through Asiatic Turkey to Basra. The project contemplates hereafter a prolongation of the line from Basra through Persia and Baluchistan, but at present the scheme would complete the communication with India by steamers from the mouth of the Euphrates down the Persian Gulf. Mr. Stephenson desires to elicit from the Government of India an expression of its approval of his project, and of its readiness to render assistance in the way of surveys and otherwise. This great project is of course in the merest outline at present. It would, no doubt, be very easy to raise objections against the plan founded on the difficulty of obtaining the necessary capital, on the wide extent of country to be traversed, the natural obstacles which obstruct its surface, and the lawless and unmanageable character of a large portion of its people. I abstain from entering into any such details at present. Even after all that has been already achieved it cannot be defined or doubted that the formation and maintenance of a line of Railway from Istanbul to Basra would be a gigantic undertaking. But as little can it be doubtful that such an undertaking, once completed and reducing the distance between England and the dominions in India to little more than ten days' journey, would prove of vast national importance, and would be a great step in the progress of the world. I make no question that the Government of India will be prepared to express to that extent its approval of Mr. Stephenson's project and that it will be willing to state its readiness at the proper time to give such assistance in respect of surveys and otherwise as its authority and the means at its command may enable it to contribute.

In the 1840s, a priori, it was impossible to determine which idea was wild. The Western Ghats between Bombay and the Deccan were a bit of a problem, and there was no dearth of novel ideas. For instance, there was Colonel J.P.

Kennedy, who was instrumental in building the Grand Hindustan and Tibet Road up to Shimla between 1849 and 1852. Since he became the government railway engineer in 1850, his views on railway construction couldn't be dismissed. A subsequent consulting engineer to the government of India on railways, G.W. MacGeorge, wrote,

> Amongst the most prominent of the many elaborate and startling theories broached on the eve of Indian railway construction was one which emanated from Colonel Kennedy, R.E.; for a short time Consulting Engineer to the Government of India for Railways, and subsequently Consulting Engineer to the Bombay, Baroda and Central India Railway Company. In a report or memorandum written at the close of the year 1851, addressed to the Honourable Court of Directors, Colonel Kennedy drew up a kind of code of rules and regulations for the proposed guidance of railway authorities in India containing some essentially novel views and opinions, which, coming from a man in his prominent position, necessarily demanded attention and careful consideration. Dealing first with the military and economical aspects of the question of railways in India, Colonel Kennedy proceeded, in twelve proposed regulations, to lay down the broad general principles on which the whole railway system of the country ought, in his opinion, to be guided, and, in unsparing language, he condemned

all that had hitherto been done by railway engineers. In opposition to the contemplated direct route of the 'East Indian Railway' from Calcutta to Mirzapur, passing through the Shergotty range of hills, and the ascent of the line of Western ghats by the proposed 'Great Indian Peninsula Railway' from Bombay, he argued in favour of a sort of Median and Persian Government decree, that no trunk line of railway in India should have a ruling gradient of more than 1 foot in every 2000 feet, or 1 in 330 on secondary or branch lines; that no line should be undertaken which was estimated to cost more than 5000 a mile, exclusive of bridging the larger rivers; and in order to secure the necessary flat gradients, and on the hasty assumption that the rivers of the country were everywhere the main arteries of commerce, he proposed that lines of railway should be constructed skirting the whole coast line of India , and thence be carried all over the interior of the country by closely following the lines of the great river valleys. Thus the line of the 'East Indian Railway' should closely follow the course of the Ganges from Calcutta, via the great bend at Rajmahal; and the line of 'Great Indian Peninsula Railway' from Bombay, instead of recklessly ascending the Western ghats on a necessarily steep and most expensive alignment, should follow the natural routes to the interior in the north, via the coast line and the Tapti and Narbada valleys; and on the south to Madras, via the coast, the gap in the ghats near Coimbatore, and the

Kaveri valley to the eastern coast line. The twelve
general rules and principles advocated by Colonel
Kennedy, although in their most essential features
not adopted, had nevertheless, the advantageous
result of compelling the close attention of the
Government authorities to many matters of the
highest importance in connection with the first
location and construction of railways on a new
and virgin soil, and this manner may possibly
have hastened the arrival at precise and definite
conclusions respecting them. In the early part of
the year 1853, Lord Dalhousie, then Governor-
General of India, after having received the reports
and opinions of all the various consulting engineers
and railway experts in the country, reviewed in a
masterly minute, at once clear and exhaustive, the
whole question of railway routes for the earlier
trunk lines, and the guiding principles to be adopted
on all the main points of controversy which had
been so long under discussion.[20]

There was also Colonel Grant of the Bombay Engineers.
His interests were quite diverse. In 1854, he authored
a monograph titled, 'Indian Irrigation: being a short
description of the system of artificial irrigation and canal
navigation in India, with a proposal for carrying the same
into effect by private enterprise.' In 1838, he wrote a piece

---

[20] Quoted in 'Eminent Railwaymen of Yesteryears', R.R. Bhandari,
2008, http://www.irfca.org/articles/eminent-railwaymen.html

titled, 'On the Fact of Small Fish falling during Rain in India.' A 1850 monograph is more pertinent for our purposes. This was titled, 'Bombay Cotton and Indian Railways.'[21]

'India was a country of extremes with vast plains, high and precipitous mountain ranges, broad rivers, down which at certain seasons of the year vast volumes of water flowed with great rapidity. In England the railway passed over the undulating country facing frequent small obstacles almost at every yard. However in India the railway would pass through a plain requiring not more than the mere superficial construction of the permanent way involving an insignificant expenditure. But then it would have to ascend a range of hills or cross a vast river, which would consume a vast capital,' observed the monograph. With India's high mountains, impassable rivers, thick forests and herds of cattle and other straying animals, Colonel Grant thought that permanent railway tracks along the surface of the ground were not practical. He proposed that railway tracks should be suspended through the entire length using suspension chains, at a minimum height that was eight feet above the ground, high enough to avoid animals and also high enough to allow for a fairly uniform alignment. Extraordinary though the idea was, models of this plan were prepared and exhibited.

We should next mention Dwarakanath Tagore (1794–1846), Rabindranath Tagore's grandfather. He was a social

---

[21] *Bombay Cotton and Indian Railways*, Charles William Grant, Longman, Brown, Green and Longman, 1850.

reformer, industrialist and entrepreneur. His business interests straddled banking, insurance, shipping and trading, with a focus on items like indigo, silk, sugar and coal. With a British partner, he established Carr, Tagore and Company in 1843, an outfit that had close commercial ties with the East India Company. On a visit to England, Dwarakanath Tagore got interested in trains and wished to bring rail transportation to Bengal.

Rowland Macdonald Stephenson first arrived in Calcutta in 1843 as a representative of the Steam Navigation Company. When he and Dwarakanath Tagore met, they realized they had a common interest in developing railways in India. It wasn't Dwarakanath Tagore alone among the Indians who was interested. There were others too—Ram Comul Sen (1795/96–1844), Mutty Lall Seal (1791–1854) and Ram Gopal Ghosh (1815–68).[22] 'It was a part of Stephenson's strategy in this country to write about railways in various journals, to publish reports of the European railway companies and to write letters to the "influential" (mostly European) here, so that they could be made aware of the "benefits" of railways.'[23] At that time, Dwarakanath Tagore also owned the *Englishman*, the newspaper in which Stephenson used to articulate his views about the railways.[24] Because of his business

---

[22] See, 'The Colonial Context of the Bengal Renaissance: A Note on Early Railway-Thinking in Bengal', Dipesh Chakrabarty, *op.cit.*

[23] *Ibid.*

[24] After Dwarakanath Tagore's death, Stephenson came to own the *Englishman*.

interests, Dwarakanath Tagore wanted that there should be railways in the collieries. To push this idea, he got in touch with a friend of Stephenson's, a Calcutta-based barrister named William Theobold. If the lines were to be laid from Calcutta to the Raniganj coalfields, Dwarakanath Tagore even offered to raise one-third of the capital.

All these very different men agreed on the need for railways. Ram Comul Sen (his name is also written as Ramkamal Sen), who was more of a social reformer and author and less of an entrepreneur or industrialist, passed away in 1844. Mutty Lall Seal had business interests in real estate, and trading interests in indigo, sugar, rice, salt-petre and cotton piece-goods. He also owned ships. In 1844, Seal wrote a letter in reply to Stephenson's:

> There can be no doubt the country would be largely benefited by the introduction of railways. Whether they would pay is a question experience only can answer. My decided opinion, however, is that lines connecting our great interior marts with this city, could hardly fail to yield a large return on the original outlay . . . In fact the more I look at this subject, the more satisfied do I feel that the introduction of a well-organized system of railway communication into Bengal would prove not only highly advantageous to the Presidency itself, but also to the Shareholders, by yielding them a liberal and steady return for their capital.[25]

---

[25] Chakrabarty, *op.cit*.

Ram Gopal Ghosh too was in favour of railways. Amongst the three influential industrialists of Bengal whose advice was sought for the railway question in India, it was Ram Gopal Ghosh who raised and addressed the social changes that railways would usher in. He pointed out the concerns of general public commutation by train in the context of religious and gender prejudices. He meticulously raised all the issues that might arise or prevent Indians from travelling on the railways. Ghosh argued that for the majority of Indians, train commutation would be unaffordable. Nonetheless, the 'growing classes of intelligent natives' would prefer trains, he concluded. In a letter written to Stephenson in 1844, he wrote:

> The commercial benefits that are likely to arise from . . . railways are unquestionable and . . . almost incalculable . . . That it will benefit the country by developing her hidden and partially-opened resources—that it will infuse a spirit of enterprises hitherto unknown to her merchants—and that it will increase the consumption of British and other goods where they are known, and create a demand for them where they are not—are inferences which even the cautious must admit . . . The reasons which induce us to view the project favourably are, on the one hand, the certain cheap cost of railways in this country . . . and, on the other hand, the existence of an extensive trade between Calcutta and the Upper Provinces, which is sure to increase with the facilities

of railway communication . . . While we admit that the majority of people cannot afford to travel in a railway train, we maintain that the number of those who can are by no means small . . . and, lastly, the religious connexion between the Hindoos and the holy cities of Benaras, Gyah, Allahabad, and others, would alone fill the trains with hundreds of the better class of pilgrims. This brings us to consider the extent of religious prejudices. As a native of the land, the writer feels some confidence in stating his opinion that he believes they may be overcome by a few simple arrangements. Let there be three divisions of the people, namely, Mahomedans, and high and low caste Hindoos. If any female passengers offer, let them be accommodated in separate carriages. And do not let the travelers be required to make a run of more than twelve hours at a time.[26]

He also felt 'the civilizing influence of steam' would gradually remove many of these prejudices.

Clearly there was both a British interest and an Indian interest in railways. At that time, the president of the Bengal British India Society was William Theobald. Through him, Stephenson sought some answers from Dwarakanath Tagore:

Conformably with your wishes I have laid the letter containing your inquiries respecting the amount of

---

[26] *Ibid.*

traffic from the Burdwan collieries, and the cost of transport, before my friend Dwarakanath Tagore.[27]

Question 1: What is the extent of present trade in coal between Burdwan and Calcutta by the Damooda?

Answer: About 20 lakhs of maunds. The present collieries are capable of producing fifty.

Question 2: What amount paid for conveyance to Calcutta?

Answer: 7 rupees 8 annas per 100 maunds to Omptah=1,50,000. 2 rupees 8 annas from Omptah to Calcutta=50,000.

Question 3: What quantity lost, stolen or wasted in transits?

Answer: Twenty per cent at least.

Question 4: What would be the possible increase in trade, if increased facilities are affordable for conveyance of the coal?

Answer: Besides coal, rice, sugar, shell lac and a little indigo.

---

[27] Undated letter, cited in Chakrabarty, *op.cit*.

Question 5: What price would the coal company engage to pay per 1000 maunds for transport of coal to Calcutta?

Answer: 10 rupees per 100 maunds.

The Damooda is the Damodar river. Omptah is today's Amta. Dwarakanath Tagore formed the Bengal Coal Company in 1843, in partnership with Gilmore Hombray and Company. We have a statement on the amount of coal the Bengal Coal Company shipped from 'Raneegunge' to Omptah between October 1846 and September 1847, and that figure was 17,10,126 maunds.[28] That figure of 20 lakh maunds wasn't an overestimate.

Though there was agreement on the need for railways, agreement on railways routes was a different matter. Stephenson formed the East Indian Railway Company (EIRC) in 1845, and in the same year, Dwarakanath Tagore formed the Great Western Railway of Bengal (GWRB). The routes planned by EIRC and GWRB for the main line from Calcutta to Mirzapur were different (nothing to do with the six routes proposed by Stephenson). An article from 1845 gives us an idea of the difference between the two proposed routes:[29]

---

[28] *Partner in Empire: Dwarakanath Tagore and the Age of Enterprise in Eastern India*, Blair B. Kling, University of California Press, 1976.

[29] *Railways in India; Being Four Articles Reprinted from the Railway Register*, July–November 1845, Madden and Malcolm, London, 1845.

Mr. R.M. Stephenson's plan (we take his immediate project, without its ultimate extensions), consists in a line of railway from Calcutta—or rather from Howra on the opposite side of the river—to that important mart, Mirzapore, with a branch to Lucheron. The length of this line would be about 400 miles. It would start direct from the right bank of the Hoogly, and so through Burdwan, direct to its terminus. The Great Western Railway of Bengal takes a more northern direction. It starts from Calcutta, keeping the left bank of the Hoogly till it gets to Chogda (an important military station), where it crosses the river, and then proceeds, passing by Burdwan, Raneegunje, Kuruckdea, Behar, to Patna. From Chogda a branch proceeds more due north, by Kishnagur, Moorshedabad, to Sootee, an important commercial depôt. The total length of the line to Patna is estimated at about 320 miles, and of the branch to Sootee about 115 miles, making a total of 435 miles.

The GWRB line was a bit longer. However, there was no question that the GWRB line presented fewer engineering problems. 'Upon the whole, therefore, in an engineering point of view, we think there can be little doubt that the Great Western of Bengal is the preferable scheme of the two which we have named.'[30] This particular article also sought to estimate revenue from freight, not so much

---

[30] *Ibid.*

passenger, traffic along these two lines. However, probably because of difficulties of estimating future revenue, that criterion wasn't used by the article to favour one route over the other. The debate continued.[31]

The route eventually chosen wasn't quite exactly either of the original two proposed. But more importantly, the EIRC was preferred over the GWRB. This wasn't a decision based entirely on railway considerations. It was very unlikely that a company under 'native' management would be allowed to construct such an important railway line. In other business areas, Dwarakanath Tagore's commercial interests often conflicted with those of the East India Company. There were political issues too. Dwarakanath Tagore died in 1846, and the GWRB was merged with the EIRC to form the East Indian Railways (EIR).

Between 1848 and 1856, Lord Dalhousie was the Governor General. The initial development of railways in the country had a lot to do with him.

Other than Stephenson, there was another railway enthusiast in the form of John Chapman (1801–54), one of the movers, though not the only one, behind the Great Indian Peninsula Railway (GIPR).[32] In a strictly formal sense, the GIPR proposal was received before

---

[31] See, *Communication and Colonialism in Eastern India: Bihar, 1760s–1880s,* Nitin Sinha, Anthem Press, 2012.

[32] See, 'John Chapman and the Promotion of the Great Indian Peninsular Railway, 1842–1850', Ian J. Kerr in Ralf Roth and Gunter Dinhobl edited, *Across the Borders. Financing the World's Railways in the Nineteenth and Twentieth Centuries*, Ashgate Publishing, 2008.

Stephenson's, and that initial proposal was extremely ambitious, linking large parts of the country that were certain to be unviable, commercially as well as politically.

There was the EIRC, incorporated in 1845, and there was the GIPR, also incorporated in 1845. However, 1845 wasn't the year they got permissions to build. That happened later. And, since the EIRC and the GIPR drove those initial lines, the connections were from east to north and from west to north. The rest of India was relatively ignored.

EIRC logo   **GIPR logo**

The Court of Directors of the East India Company posed some questions to the Governor General.[33] What about periodical rains and inundations, continued action of violent winds and the influence of a vertical sun, the ravages of insects and vermin, the destructive growth of spontaneous vegetation of underwood upon earth

---

[33] See, *Development of Indian Railways*, Nalinaksha Sanyal, University of Calcutta, 1930.

and brickwork, the unenclosed and unprotected tracts of country through which the railroad would pass, and the difficulty and expense of securing the services of competent and trustworthy engineers? How would these problems be handled?

Frederick James Halliday (1806–1901) had a role to play in the development of the railways. He became Secretary to the Board of Revenue in 1836, Secretary to the government of India in 1849 and the first Lieutenant Governor of Bengal in 1854. Aware of the various proposals floating around, in 1845 he suggested to the Court of Directors of the East India Company to send him an expert. This expert would examine the feasibility of railway lines and draw up plans for building them. In a way, this was the first time the Court of Directors had officially acknowledged the desirability of railways in India and invited the opinion of the government of India on the construction of lines, the terms under which they would be constructed and the role of the state. At the time, there were two main concerns.[34] First, given religious and caste biases, would Indians take to travel by rail? Second, with India's specific climatic and geographical conditions, could railways be built? With the benefit of hindsight, both these apprehensions were unwarranted. But that's not the way it looked in 1845 or 1849. The Court of Directors took the subject seriously and sent Halliday an engineer named Frederick Walter Simms (1803–65). Simms was a surveyor

---

[34] *The Railways of India: With an Account of Their Rise, Progress and Construction,* Edward Davidson, E. & F.N. Spon, London, 1868.

and civil engineer who was subsequently employed by
the South Eastern Railway Company in Britain. He
patented and pioneered the use of asphalt and road tracts
on tunnelling. In 1846, the East India Company appointed
Simms as a consulting engineer. This suggested that the
East India Company had tentatively decided to push for
railway construction in India.

This background to the development of Indian
Railways deserves to be run through again.[35] In Madras
Presidency, proposals for railways surfaced in the 1830s,
and Arthur Cotton submitted one for a Madras–Bombay
line in 1836. There was the Stephenson proposal, linking
Calcutta with the North-West Frontier areas, eventually
culminating in the EIRC. In Bombay, there was a proposal
for a Bombay Great Eastern Railway, with 'Thull and
Bhore Ghat roads for crossing the mountain barriers to
the east of Bombay. The Governor of Bombay received
the suggestions with sympathy and had a preliminary
survey made by the military engineer officers.'[36]

'In November 1844, Messrs. White Borret &
Company, on behalf of the "Great Indian Railway
Company" approached the Court of Directors with a
proposal to construct a trunk line across the Deccan with
branches to the north and south.'[37]

Given all these proposals, Simms was entrusted
with the task of investigating the following. With India's

---

[35] See the discussion in *Development of Indian Railways*, Nalinaksha
Sanyal, University of Calcutta, 1930.
[36] *Ibid.*
[37] *Ibid.*

special conditions, could railway development handle (1) periodical rains and inundations; (2) the continued action of violent winds and the influence of a vertical sun; (3) the ravages of insects and vermin; (4) the destructive growth of spontaneous vegetation of underwood upon earth and brick-work; (5) the unenclosed and unprotected tracts of country through which railroads would pass; (6) the difficulty and expense of securing the services of competent and trustworthy engineers?[38] Plus, would Indians take to the railways? Simms was also supposed to recommend which lines would be chosen for construction. In 1846, Simms submitted a report favouring the development of railways in India. In so far as the questions above were concerned, there were other favourable reports too.

However, there were other important questions to be addressed. Who would build the railway lines? There was no ambiguity on this. The railways would be built by the private sector. Who would acquire the land? That would clearly have to be acquired by the government and handed over to the companies on lease, with the land reverting to the government after the lease period was over (these are issues we are grappling with even today). But would this be enough? After all, the government would reap positive externalities from the railways. The capital couldn't be raised in India. It would have to be raised in England. Without some kind of capital contribution from the government, would the venture be attractive enough? Should there be some kind of guarantee system? What

---

[38] *Ibid.*

figure would suffice for guarantee? What capital base
would that guarantee figure be worked out on, and would
there be some estimate of how much (per mile) railway
construction would cost? How would profits be shared
between the company and the government? There were
protracted correspondence and negotiations over such
issues. In addition, 'Recommendations were also made at
the time about future Government proprietorship, steps to
be taken in case of failure of maintenance or construction,
strict supervision and control by the State, free carriage
of mails, conveyance of Government traffic, civil and
military, at reduced rates, and preparation of accounts
and statistics and submission thereof for inspection. The
railway companies were to be free from the payment of
any duties and taxes, and would exercise complete control
over their servants.'[39] Time was lost in the process, and
because capital market conditions worsened, this meant
the government had to accept a larger burden as the
guaranteed rate of interest increased during that delay.
Finally, in 1849, there were agreements between the East
India Company and the EIRC and the GIPR.

The resultant guarantee system has been criticized
almost universally.

> The substance of the first agreements was that the
> Government relieved the shareholders of all risk,
> gave them some expectation of profit over and
> above the guaranteed interest, and claimed in return

---

[39] Sanyal, *op.cit.*

reasonable powers of control and ultimate right of purchase. The principal defects in the contracts lay in making no provision for the State's participation in the profits, in permitting a fixed rate of exchange to govern the transactions, in allowing the guarantee to run from the day of deposit of money and not from the date of opening of the lines, in providing little check on the capital expenditure of the companies, and in granting the private enterprisers opportunities for enjoying the full benefit of unearned increment in the value of the property when the time for the State purchase of the railways came.[40]

Specifically, this is what the agreements said: (1) a contract for ninety-nine years, with an interest guaranteed for all money paid into the government treasury and for the entire period; (2) the amount advanced as guarantee was to be repaid from profits; (3) after twenty-five or fifty years, the government could purchase the railway back at the mean (over the preceding three years) market value of those shares in London, though railway companies could surrender the lines whenever they wanted, claiming the amount spent as lump sum or annuities; (4) land for railway lines and all other works would be provided free by the government; (5) routes, gauge, constructions, gradients and all alterations had to be sanctioned and approved by the government; (6) the government retained powers of control and supervision and free access to account books,

[40] *Ibid.*

with the power to approve fares and reduce them in some situations; (7) there would be a government director with veto powers on all railway boards of directors; (8) mail and postal servants would be carried free while troops and military stores would be carried at reduced rates; (9) the exchange rate used for conversions would be 1s. 10d. per rupee; and (9) depending on the money market, the rate of interest would vary between 4.5 per cent and 5 per cent. However, this was the first round of guarantees, modified a bit later.

All this was about the EIRC and the GIPR. What about the Madras proposals? They were initially delayed because no joint stock company had been contemplated. That idea took off a little later, as did the Bombay Baroda and Central India Railway.

3

THE 1850S AND 1860S: EXPANSION

Everyone has heard of Lord Dalhousie. But not too many people have heard of Krishna Shastri Bhatwadekar (also spelt Bhatawadekar). What is remarkable is that in 1854, Bhatwadekar authored a book in Marathi on railways. In English, this is titled *A Short Account of Railways,* and there is a copy at the National Library, Calcutta. A book on railways had just been published, in 1850, by Dionysius Lardner.[41] Krishna Shastri Bhatwadekar's book drew heavily on Lardner. Nevertheless, it is quite remarkable that such a book was written and published in 1854, that too in Marathi.

---

[41] *Railway Economy: A Treatise on the New Art of Transport, its Management, Prospects and Relations*, Dionysius Lardner, Harper and Brothers, New York, 1850.

Illustration from Bhatwadekar's book

What about Lord Dalhousie? He became Governor General in 1848, and remained Governor General till 1856. In 1850, he wrote a Minute to the Court of Directors of the East India Company on the introduction of railways. This covered every possible issue one could think of about railways at the time. This Minute deserves extensive quoting from, but should not be confused with a subsequent Minute of 20 April 1853.[42] The 4 July 1850 Minute was primarily about what the EIRC should do.

> The capital which has been provided for the formation of the line amounts only to one million sterling, and in the contract made between the Hon'ble East India Company and the East Indian Railway Company it is specifically determined that such line shall be commenced at or within ten miles of the town of Calcutta; so that it may hereafter form part

---

[42] It has forty-seven paragraphs and is dated 4 July 1850. It has been reprinted in Roopa Srinivasan, Manish Tiwari and Sandeep Silas, *op. cit.*

of a line either to Mirzapore or to Rajamahal. I beg respectfully to express my regrets that the Hon'ble Court of Directors should have left no discretion to the Government of India as to the district in which the important experiment with which it is charged should first be instituted . . . In my humble judgement the experiment would have been commenced with better prospect of ultimate success in a different portion of the country, over which the Great Trunk Line of Railway was originally proposed to extend. The line of country above the city of Allahabad is peculiarly fitted for the successful prosecution of a Railway line. It presents few, if any engineering difficulties; it is not subject to the general inundation which covers the plains of lower Bengal; there are few river crossings and no hills. The outlay over the formation of such a railway over such a country would comparatively have been smaller in amount and the limited capital at command would have thus provided a much greater extent of line than it can supply in the province of Bengal. The execution of the line would have proceeded speedily, and return upon the outlay would have been earlier received; while the circumstances of the country through which the Railway would have passed, afford at least as good a prospect of return upon the capital invested, as the line which has now been selected . . . The object of that experiment is to prove not only that it is practicable to construct railways in India as engineering works but that such railways when constructed will, as commercial undertaking afford a fair remunerative return on the money which has been expended in their construction, so that the public may thereby be encouraged to invest their capital in the construction of similar work in other parts of India . . . I have the honour of submitting the following proposal for an experimental line, as the one which appears to me to be the best calculated for obtaining the several objects which the Court of Directors have had in view. I propose that line of railway shall be constructed from Howrah on the right bank of the Hooghly to the coal fields at or near to Raneegunge. On this and on every other occasion land should be taken in sufficient for the formation of a double line of railway, if at any time it should be found necessary or expedient. The line proceeding to Serampore, Chinsurah and Hooghly shall be carried in the direction of Burdwan to such a point, as may leave it open to the Government to select hereafter the further line direct to Mirzapore or to Rajmahal without any sacrifice of railway already constructed . . . After reading everything that I have seen written on the subject, and conversing, since I have been in India, with everybody who was able to give an opinion worth having on the question of Railways in India, I have come to the conclusion that no one yet can safely say whether Railways in this country will pay or not . . . The British Legislature fell unconsciously and perhaps unavoidably, into the mischievous error of permitting the introduction of two gauges into the United Kingdom . . . The Government of India has it in its power, and no doubt will carefully provide that,

> however widely the railway system may be extended in
> this Empire in the time to come, these great evils shall
> be averted, and that the uniformity of the gauge shall be
> rigidly enforced from the first.

There was no standardization of gauge across the early British collieries, and these gauges were what the initial railway gauge for public lines came to be based on. There was a range from 1219 mm to 1524 mm. Cross-country, gauges are still not standardized. In India, broad gauge is 1676 mm (5 ft 6 inches), metre gauge 1000 mm (3 ft 3 ³/₈ inches) and narrow gauge is 610 mm (2 ft) or 762 mm (2 ft 6 inches). In Britain, there was a Royal Commission on Railway Gauges in 1845, leading to a Gauge Act.

In that 1850 Minute, Lord Dalhousie suggested a gauge that would be between 4 ft 8½ inches and 7 ft.

This is a cliched claim that floats around freely, especially on the Net. For transport, the Romans used chariots yoked to two horses. The chariots created ruts on the roads. If a chariot's width didn't match the rut exactly, it keeled over. Thus it was that standardization came about among all those chariots, measured as the distance between the wheels. The Romans built roads all over England, according to the distance between those ruts. The horse-drawn tramways and horse-drawn railways in the collieries also stuck to the same width. Keeping this distance as the standard, the railways too developed the standard gauge of four feet and 8.5 inches (1435 mm), the same gauge also getting transported to the US. Years and years later, when space shuttles had solid rocket boosters (SRBs) that had to be transported, it had to be kept in mind that railway tunnels were a fixed percentage wider than the tracks that pass through them. And the SRBs had to be manufactured to a size that could pass through such tunnels. Therefore, it is said, the design of a space shuttle was based on the backsides of two Roman horses! In its several details that we needn't get into, this yarn isn't true, rollicking good though it reads. There was no standardization of gauge across those early British collieries. There was a range though, from 1219 mm to 1524 mm. Indeed, George Stephenson did base the gauge of his Stockton and Darlington Railway on the width of horse-drawn carts used in the collieries. (There was the father, George Stephenson, and the son, Robert Stephenson.) But that gauge was 1422 mm, not 1435 mm. He tried out 1435 mm on the Liverpool and Manchester Railway and found that to be better on curves. Thus the switch to 1435 mm, but only on the railways Stephenson built, and on those that came somewhat later.

In 1845, in the UK, there was a Royal Commission on Railway Gauges. This led to a Gauge Act. There were too many gauges floating around: 1435 mm, 2134 mm, and narrow gauges. But despite the Act, there was still incomplete standardization in the UK and the US. For instance, in the US, there was greater standardization in the north than in the south, and this inefficiency in managing its railway networks was cited as a reason for the Confederacy's defeat. If one leaves narrow and metre gauge aside, there is standard gauge (1435 mm) and broad gauge. But broad gauge also differs across countries.

India has 1676 mm, but the range across countries varies from 1520 mm to 2140 mm. There were differences within Europe too, and the European Union (EU) struggled quite a bit with gauge unification.

Both Lord Dalhousie and F. W. Simms, the consulting engineer for the East India Company, wanted a gauge broader than 1435 mm. Lord Dalhousie wanted 1829 mm and Simms favoured 1676 mm. Why couldn't India have adhered to 1435 mm? East India Company directors had a curious worry—'the continued action of violent winds, and the influence of the vertical sun'! These climatic conditions would make 1435 mm unsuitable. And despite Lord Dalhousie's preference for a uniform gauge, that didn't materialize. Narrow and metre gauge proliferated, primarily because of lower costs.

There is an apocryphal account of how Lord Mayo (Viceroy from 1869 to 1872) made three Indian males sit next to each other, measured the width of seat they occupied, and thus decided the metre gauge width. But this account is probably in the same genre as the one about the Roman horses. Under the Indian Railways' (IR) plan of gauge conversion, Project Unigauge, all narrow and metre gauge lines are now being converted into broad gauge. But this is today. Let us go back to the past.

The 1853 Dalhousie Minute was the edifice on which the railway system came to be built. The proposed network was similar to the one Stephenson proposed in 1844, but it also emphasized the Calcutta–North Western Territories link Kennedy had mentioned:

> . . . [T]he railway I referred to would be of
> incalculable value . . . Touching every military station
> from Calcutta to the Sutlej, connecting every depot,
> Allahabad, Agra, Delhi, Ferozepore, with the arsenal
> of Fort William; it would enable the Government
> of India to assemble upon [both] frontier[s] . . .
> an amount of men and materials of war amply
> sufficient to deal with any such emergency within a
> period which would be measured by days; whereas
> months must elapse, with our present means.[43]

He had also said,

> [A] single cast upon the map recalling to mind the
> vast extent of the Empire we hold . . . will suffice to
> show how immeasurable are the political advantages
> to be derived from a system of communication
> which would admit of full intelligence of every
> event being transmitted to the government under
> all circumstances, at a speed exceeding five-fold its
> present rate.

What this meant was railway construction on a grand
scale, using trunk routes, not in small bits and pieces.
This fitted with Dalhousie's vision of engines of social
improvement, meaning, the railways and postal and
telegraph services. Dalhousie was the one who first
authorized a pilot telegraph line in Calcutta, thereafter
extended to the rest of India.

---

[43] http://www.essaysinhistory.com/articles/2011/5

The Court of Directors agreed that there should be trunk lines in all three Presidencies (Bengal, Bombay and Madras). The contracts with the EIRC and the GIPR were redone so that there would be a railway line from Raichur to northern India.[44] The four approved major trunk routes were: (1) Calcutta–Delhi and onwards to Lahore/the North West Frontiers; (2) Bombay–Delhi; (3) Madras–West Coast/Malabar; and (4) Bombay Baroda and Central Indian Railway. It was also contemplated that the Calcutta–Delhi line would meet the Bombay–Delhi line at some point, yet unspecified. This leads to a very obvious point that is sometimes ignored, though it left a legacy. At no point, at least then, was a Calcutta–Madras line contemplated. Nor were there plans for a line from the central parts of India extending to the south-east. When we earlier hinted that parts of the country were bypassed, this is what we meant.

First Passenger Train

Courtesy National Rail Museum, Delhi

---

[44] Sanyal, *op.cit.*

Before 1853 and before being used on the Bori Bunder–Thane haul, there were other locomotives of the steam variety too. One such locomotive was the Thomason, as it came to be known in India. The locomotive was named after James Thomason, who was the Lieutenant Governor of the North Western Provinces between 1843 and 1853. He also had a college named after him—the Thomason College of Civil Engineering, as it was called between 1853 and 1948. It was set up in 1847, but came to be named after Thomason in 1853. This college later became the University of Roorkee, which, even later, became the Indian Institute of Technology, Roorkee. This was part of the Ganges Canal, an anti-famine irrigation and navigation waterworks programme. Thomason College was set up to supply canal engineers for the Ganges Canal project. In 1851, India's first aqueduct, the Solani viaduct or aqueduct (near Roorkee) was being constructed. The construction material for the canal was first hauled by men and then by horses, until a steam locomotive was thought of. In 1847, E.B. Wilson and Company of Leeds built ten engines of the locomotives known as Jenny Lind, named after the famous opera singer. In a sense, this was the first instance of mass production of locomotives, and the Jenny Linds were so successful that many more were built. One such Jenny Lind was imported in knocked-down condition to Calcutta, brought to Roorkee, reassembled there, and renamed Thomason. It couldn't haul more than two wagons at a time, and had a speed of 6 km/hour. So far as one can make out from reports, it wasn't very successful. After nine months of running, the boiler exploded, and that was the end of Thomason. 'The water had been drawn off, and it was supposed that the fire had been entirely extinguished. A storm with wind brought the fire and fuel which were in the furnace, into action, and destroyed the casing together with a number of tubes, placing the locomotive completely out of use.'[45]

Courtesy Wikimedia Commons

The Jenny Lind

Other than the Thomason, there was the locomotive named Falkland. Between 1852 and 1853, the GIPR imported several locomotives from the Vulcan Foundry Ltd, a British locomotive builder. So many years down the line, it is impossible to determine precisely what was imported from the Vulcan Foundry and what was imported from elsewhere. What we do know is that the GIPR had a shunting locomotive, which subsequently

---

[45] 'Report on the Ganges Canal Works', quoted in Ashwani Lohani (ed.), *Smoking Beauties, Steam Engines of the World*, Wisdom Tree, 2009.

came to be named the Falkland, after Lord Falkland. Other locomotives were also imported. One of these was used on a trial run between Bori Bunder and Thane/Tannah in 1852. If that trial run is included, one could argue that the first passenger train in India ran in 1852 and not in 1853.

A GIPR postage stamp, brought out in 1976

Understandably, there was a race between the GIPR and the EIRC. Both wanted to be the first to start a train in India. The EIRC had been the first to establish an experimental railway line between Calcutta and Rajmahal; however, this company was plain unfortunate. Both the GIPR and the EIRC had to import locomotives and coaches. For both, locomotives and coaches were dispatched from England at around the same time, by ship. Going by reports, this is what happened: The ship carrying the locomotive, HMS *Goodwin* was misdirected to Australia and had to be rerouted to Calcutta from there. The second ship, which carried the coaches, sank at Sandheads. Here is a slightly different version. 'The opening of the railway line was delayed because of the sinking of the ship HMS "GOODWIN", bringing the railway carriages, at Sandheads and because of the over-carrying of the first locomotive to Australia. The carriages were, then, built locally in Calcutta and the locomotive was received *via* Australia in 1854.'[46] The carriages being built in Calcutta is clear enough. But there seem to have been two ships, each carrying one locomotive. The first ship sank, taking down with it the locomotive. The second ship, carrying the second locomotive, went off to Australia and reached Calcutta after a long detour. In the process, the EIRC lost out. There was more trouble for the company. There was a dispute over the French territory of Chandernagore/Chandannagar, through which the line would have to pass. The EIRC's first passenger train ran on 15 August 1854, plying a distance of thirty-eight km, between Howrah and Hooghly, a line extended thereafter to Pundooah. In 1855, an experimental line was laid up to Raneegunje.

[46] *Railway Administration and Management*, J.M. Ovasdi, Deep and Deep Publications, New Delhi, 1990, citing *Indian Railways: One Hundred Years*, 1853 to 1953, Jogendra Nath Sahni, Ministry of Railways, 1953.

Courtesy IRFCA

In chapter 1, we reproduced a postage stamp issued in 1953. It is worth reproducing it again here. The EIRC's initial locomotives were imported from Kitson, Thompson and Hewitson, and two of these turned up in 1855. At first they were simply numbered 21 and 22. Later, they were referred to as EIR 91 and EIR 92. It was only much later, in 1895, that they came to acquire the respective names of the Express and the Fairy Queen. The old locomotive shown in the postage stamp is the Express. It is believed to have been the locomotive that was used for the Howrah–Hooghly train. Evidently, it was also used for ferrying British troops to suppress the 1857 War of Independence. Subsequently, the Express retired and was preserved at the Jamalpur Locomotive Workshop (more on Jamalpur later). It then became an exhibit at the Railway Museum, Howrah. However, it was subsequently restored in 2010 by the

Perambur Locomotive Works and used to haul the Heritage Express.

The documentation available on the early locomotives isn't particularly good. The Express and the Fairy Queen are commonly believed to be sister locomotives, both built by Kitson, Thompson and Hewitson. But there also seems to be a view that the Express was built by Stothert, Slaughter and Company of Bristol, and not by Kitson, Thompson and Hewitson. It shouldn't be that difficult to resolve this anomaly. As for the Fairy Queen, it is a famous locomotive. It was withdrawn from service in 1909. But, restored in 1997, it did a two-day excursion from Delhi to Alwar, with an overnight stay in Sariska. That train was called the Fairy Queen Express, and the locomotive entered the Guinness World Records as the oldest functional steam locomotive in the world. For reasons not clear, the locomotive was withdrawn (parts were probably stolen) and it is now housed in the Rewari steam locomotive shed. The Delhi–Alwar train is still operated by Indian Railway Catering and Tourism Corporation (IRCTC). But with the Fairy Queen gone, it can no longer be called the Fairy Queen Express. It's called the Steam Express and its locomotive is a WP 7161. For years, WP was the workhorse of the railways in India. 'W' signifies a broad gauge locomotive, and 'P' signifies that it is used for passenger traffic. WP 7161 is indigenous (the initial WPs were imported) and was built at Chittaranjan Locomotive Works. It is the engine we saw in the film *Bhaag Milkha Bhaag*. WP 7161 has a name—Akbar. But no one seems to refer to it as Akbar. It is generally called WP 7161.

Courtesy IRFCA by George Woods

The restored Fairy Queen

Initially, the locomotives of those times were imported.

. . . Much of what went into India's railways: locomotives, equipment, steel for bridges and structures, rails, and sleepers, were almost entirely sourced from outside the country. While over time, some of the simpler items of these—sleepers, bolts et cetera began to be indigenously manufactured, the more technology-intensive in this list, locomotives for instance, continued to be imported chiefly from Great Britain. Attempts at locomotive production domestically, in the initial years, were thwarted or at least inhibited, by the adoption of 'standard types' of locomotives, which meant that special sanction was needed to build 'non-standard' locomotives. However, there were some definite spin-offs— railway technology requires extensive facilities for repair and maintenance, almost at the same scale as for manufacture. Therefore, quite early on, India's railway network saw the fairly extensive development of workshops, sheds and shops for repair and maintenance of rolling stock.[47]

Between 1853 and 1947, 14,400 locomotives were imported from Great Britain, and around 3000 locomotives from other countries. Between 1865 and 1941, India produced 700 locomotives.

This brings us to Jamalpur. The Jamalpur Railway Workshop was established in 1860. It is impossible to overlook Jamalpur when it comes to the history of Indian Railways. This was where the EIRC established its first railway workshop, in 1862. Why was Jamalpur, adjacent to Munghyr (Munger) chosen? For years, even centuries, Munger had been a centre for the manufacture of guns— not only legal weapons, but also guns of the illegal and cottage variety. That's a standard reason given for the choice of Munger—its tradition of making guns, pistols, spears and other ironware. Another reason advanced was that a railway line being attempted between Howrah and Delhi might pass through Munger/Jamalpur. But a shorter line (the Grand Chord or main line) developed via Gaya/Mughal Sarai and the entire so-called Sahibganj Loop, including Munger/Jamalpur, became relatively

---

[47] Introduction in Roopa Srinivasan, Manish Tiwari and Sandeep Silas, *op. cit.*

neglected. Munger/Jamalpur were on the longer Sahibganj Loop and when the decision about Jamalpur was taken, the construction of the Grand Chord had not been anticipated. No doubt, each of these reasons contains some element of truth, but there is another story too. Most of the employees in the railway workshop then were English. They preferred hotels, restaurants and billiard-rooms to the Howrah workshop, and so long as the workshop was in Howrah, they were found more in these places of entertainment than in the workshop, even during working hours. Hence the workshop was shifted from Howrah to Jamalpur, more than 450 km away. Rudyard Kipling visited Jamalpur in 1888 and wrote three pieces (not very charitable) on his visit in the *Pioneer*. They were published under the series 'Among the Railway Folk'.[48] His descriptions also covered the workshop:

> Walk into a huge, brick-built, tin-roofed stable, capable of holding twenty-four locomotives under treatment, and see what must be done to the Iron Horse, once every three years if he is to do his work well. On reflection, Iron Horse is wrong. An engine is a she—as distinctly feminine as a ship or a mine.

As the examples of the Express and the Fairy Queen indicate, locomotives weren't initially given names.

---

[48] https://ebooks.adelaide.edu.au/k/kipling/rudyard/railway/chapter1.html

They were only distinguished by numbers, whether they were imported or domestically manufactured, as they subsequently were. Eventually, names began to be used, mostly the names of British bureaucrats or railway engineers—Lord Irwin, Lord Reading, Lord Elgin, Lord Harding, Lord Minto. The sole exception at the time was a locomotive named after Ramgotty Mukherjee, the last general manager of the Nalhati–Azimganj light railway (more on it later in the book). Almost certainly, this was the first locomotive named after an Indian, and it was built in 1862 by Anjubault, the French manufacturer. Down the years, the EIRC was always innovative in naming its locomotives, though the christening of locomotives was now no longer taken as seriously as it used to be earlier. For instance, the EIRC started the business of naming locomotives after insects—the gnat, locust, ant, hornet, bee, cricket, etc., or after animals and birds—deer, fox, monkey, eagle, etc. The Ramgotty locomotive is now housed at the National Railway Museum, Delhi. After the initial years, all locomotives were christened, especially during the steam era. That's become rare now. The last steam locomotive built (in 1970) was named Antim Sitara. Oddly enough, despite being built as late as in 1970, no one knows where this locomotive is now. Sure, diesel and electric locomotives are also occasionally named, often after political leaders—Lokmanya, Jagjivan Ram, Baba Saheb, Jawahar, Lal Bahadur Shastri, Deshbandhu. But no one takes these names seriously any more. Even if the names are mounted above the buffers when a locomotive is first built, subsequently, after several visits to workshops, the name boards vanish. Thus, locomotives have become anonymous.

Courtesy Wikimedia Commons

The Ramgotty locomotive

The 1857 War of Independence was a bit of a watershed for several reasons. After the Bori Bunder–Thane line, the GIPR opened the Khandala–Pune line in 1858. Bits and pieces were added to this gradually. Kalyan was called Callian in those days. The 1854 Thane–Kalyan extension was relatively easy, since this was only up to the foothills of the Western Ghats. From Kalyan, one line would extend to the north-east, towards Kasara (Kassarah then).[49] Another line would extend towards the

---

[49] See, 'Romancing the Bhore Ghat', Ashish P. Kuvelkar, in *More Miles . . . More Smiles*, Ministry of Railways and Railway Board, 2014.

south-east, to Khopoli (Campoolie then). By 1856, the line up to Khopoli was ready. With the Khandala–Pune line also laid, if one could merely link Pune with Khandala, travel between Bombay and Poona would become so much easier. However, this involved traversing the Western Ghats. More specifically, it involved negotiating a twenty-one km stretch known as the Bhor/Bhore Ghat section between Khandala and Palasdari, cutting across the Sahyadri range. From an engineering point of view, the problem was solved by constructing a reversing station. When this stretch of line was modernized in 1929, the reversing station was no longer needed and was scrapped. But back then,

> It took about seven long years to lay this 15-mile railway line as thousands of men worked tirelessly without the aid of modern machinery to bore long tunnels through the mountains and to build high bridges across the many ravines in the ghats. Hundreds died in construction accidents or in cholera epidemics but they persevered against all odds. Climbing some of the stiff cliffs was next to impossible, so workers had to be suspended by ropes to be able to drill holes and blast cuttings in the jagged rocks. After the line was commissioned in 1863, the rail journey from Bombay to Poona could be completed in about six hours—quite an achievement for that era.[50]

---

[50] *Ibid.*

The famous Marathi novelist Shubhada Gogate authored an award-winning novel, *Khandalyachya Ghatasathi,* in 1992. Though it was a work of fiction, it was based on the experience of negotiating the Bhor Ghat. As for the other stretch, the Kasara line was completed in 1861. However, one still needed to negotiate another ghat through the Western Ghats, the Kasara Ghat, or the Thal/Thul Ghat. Once this was completed in 1865, the GIPR could claim that it had crossed the Sahyadris.

In the south, the Madras Railway Company was formed in 1852. (It is sometimes reported that the first general body meeting of the Madras Railway Company was held in London in February 1846. That must have been a preliminary meeting, since the date of incorporation is beyond doubt.) In this context, one has to digress now to the subject of a rather interesting Bill drafted by the UK Law Commission in 2012.[51] This was designed to repeal old statutes, and was based on a joint report by the UK Law Commission and the Scottish Law Commission. The bill contained an entire section on railway companies in India and Pakistan.

> The combination of gradual nationalization and acquisition of state independence means that the individual railway companies have all now disappeared, and the UK legislation required for their formation and running has long been superseded. As a consequence, the 38 Acts relating

[51] www.gov.uk/government/uploads/system/uploads/attachment_ data/file/228649/8330.pdf

to the various railway companies (and now recited in
the draft Bill), spanning nearly a century of railway
endeavour, are recommended for repeal as obsolete.

In that list of legislation, one finds mention of the Assam
Railways and Trading Company (1881), the Bengal and
North Western Railway Company (1882), the Bombay
Baroda and Central India Railway Company (1855), the
Calcutta and South Eastern Railway Company (1857),
the East Indian Railway Company (1845), the East Bengal
Railway Company (1855), the Great Indian Peninsula
Railway Company (1849), the Madras Railway Company
(1852), the Oude Railway Company (1856), the Scinde
Railway Company (1855) and the South Indian Railway
Company (1857). This gives a reasonably good idea of what
was going on, at least in terms of the railway companies being
formed, if not of actual railway construction. From this Bill
we know the Madras Railway Company was going to build
a line from Madras to Arcot, with branches to Bangalore
and the 'Neilgherries', eventually linking up, via Bellary, the
line from Bombay. The Royapuram (Chennai)–Arcot line
was opened in 1856 (this would help connect to Bangalore
and Bombay), the line to Beypore in 1862 and the link to
Bangalore Cantonment in 1864. The Royapuram railway
station was opened in 1856, and is both an architectural
wonder and a heritage structure. It is the oldest station in
India that is still operational. There were older stations in
Bombay and Thane, but those are no longer operational.

Since the Scinde Railway Company has been
mentioned, a word now on what is probably well known:

As mentioned, the Scinde Railway Company was formed in 1855. Earlier, Karachi was only a fishing village. As the Commissioner of Sind, Henry Edward Frere sought permission from Lord Dalhousie to build Karachi into a port and to build a railway line from Karachi to Kotri. The Indus–Sarasvati civilization hadn't quite been 'discovered' then. That would start to happen, in the 1870s. But in the 1850s, the railway engineers, John and William Brunton, started to construct the Karachi–Lahore railway line, and required ballast for the tracks. They found bricks in two ancient and ruined cities, Brahminabad and Harappa. The Indus–Sarasvati civilization bricks were thus used to stabilize and support two sections of the Karachi–Lahore line. Here is an interesting quotation from John Brunton:

> The natives of Scinde had never *seen* a Locomotive Engine, they had heard of them as dragging great loads on the lines by some hidden power they could not understand, therefore they feared them, supposing that they moved by some diabolical agency, they called them Shaitan (or Satan). During the Mutiny the Mutineers got possession of one of the East Indian Line Stations where stood several Engines. They did not dare approach them but stood a good way off and threw stones at them![52]

---

[52] *John Brunton's Book Being the Memories of John Brunton, Engineer, from a Manuscript in His Own Hand Written for his Grandchildren and Now First Printed*, Cambridge University Press, 1939.

Barwarie is a village 23 miles from Allahabad. There is a railway water tank there 16 ft high and 23 ft long and 24 ft broad and 4 ft deep. On Sunday 7th June, 1857 at noon day after the massacre at Allahabad, P. O. Snow railway engineer, Mr Mathers, Mr Leithbridge with wife and child, Mr Keymer were all with wife and child, Mr Keymer were all with wife and 3 kids, Mrs R. Keymer were all employed in the railway and Major and Mrs Ryoes were all assembled at the latter's bungalow at Barwarie when information came that Mr Lancaster, an inspector had been murdered a mile off when trying to join the above party. Immediately on getting this news Mrs Ryoes the woman and kids were assisted up to the top of the railway water tank for safety but men came down for food provisions etc but an immense crowd of armed natives began to assemble near the water tank. The men therefore thought it to be prudent to stay on the water tank lest they be killed. The natives commenced looting the furniture in the bungalow of T.J. Ryes—a correspondent from Allahabad, who later reported this incident to the Illustrated London News of 2 January, 1858. After destruction they burnt down the house and outhouses. They rushed and surrounded the railway water tank by hundreds throwing brickbats and stones on the British and their families perched on the tank. The British retaliated with the fire of their guns they had. The tank was not covered and therefore the women and kids had to be protected by a mattress. They demanded money too which was thrown at them apparently to keep them at bay. When the natives realized the stranded British had no more to give (having thrown them Rs 3000/-) they asked them to come down. The British naturally refused to oblige. Then they brought straw and other inflammable material and piled them around the tank and set fire to it whose heavy smoke and heat troubled the people on the tank. Finding all their exertions over they said they would spare them if all of them—the British came down and became 'Mahometans'. This of course was refused by all. The British shouted back that all the members were prepared to die protecting their women and children. They retaliated that they were gathering a larger force of armed people to kill them soon. They were 14 British on the water tank. They were suffering badly in the hot sun without any water to drink. They had only boiled rice and parched grain to eat against about 3000 armed members of the revolt. They had provisions for about 52 hours. On the evening of 8th June Mr Smith an inspector tried to join their party he was seriously wounded so he ran for his life along with another inspector Thomas. Thomas was later murdered when he tried to rejoin the stranded party on the tank. Mr Smith was pulled up the tank with the help of ropes. He was fifteenth person of the party then. He had been wounded and was weak and in bad shape so hardly of any help to those who had pulled him up and saved him. Having succeeded in sending a message through a servant to the Commanding Officer at the Fort at Allahabad telling them of their position and condition a relief of 35 Irregular Cavalry were set out to rescue the British. They arrived at about 4 p.m.

on the 9th of June. Seeing them they shrieked to thank God and lustily cheer the troops who had been sent for their succour. The distress of women and kids without conveniences was pitiable. One of the woman Mrs Ryoes was killed by the heat and exhaustion on the tank. She died an hour after the arrival of the relief adding to the long list of deaths covered by the rebellion all over Allahabad and other places. The villagers headed by the zamindars were the people who looted, destroyed and burnt all the railway gentlemen's bungalows on the line. But the East Indian Railway water tank was thus defended and saved by the British until a relief saved them too after 32 hours.[53]

There were many dislocations during 1857. For instance, all railway construction buildings near cantonments were converted into fortified military posts. The main terminal in Charbagh in Lucknow was converted in such a way as to house the entire European population of the city in the event of an evacuation.

1857 caught the British unawares, and there was criticism that had railway construction proceeded according to schedule, British defence and security interests could have been ensured more satisfactorily. In his Appendix to his Monograph published in 1857 by Hyde Clarke, a railway economist and editor of the *Railway Times*, he reproduced

---

[53] *The Illustrated London News*, 2 January 1858, reproduced in www.railwaysofraj.blogspot.in. This is the village now known as Garhi Barwari, in Mathura district.

a letter he had written on 7 July 1857 to the *Times*, titled 'Railways and Indian Revolts'. In the letter, he writes:

> The late disastrous events in India have produced a very powerful effect on the Indian Railway department, and the authorities are pledged to the development of the railway system. Had the East Indian Railway been complete from Calcutta to Delhi, as it ought to have been, instead of halting half way, the late disastrous events at Meerut and Delhi would never have occurred, or within twenty hours troops would have been conveyed there, whereas it will now take about eighty days to march. Had the Northern Bengal Railway been complete, fresh English battalions could have been poured down from Darjeeling to Calcutta and the Valley of the Ganges; and had the Shimla Railway been complete, the Commander-in-Chief would, in six hours, have proceeded with his staff and European forces from Shimla and Soobathoo[54] to Delhi. Now, a fortnight, at least, will be spent in concentrating the requisite forces. It is expected that the salutary example of these comparisons will lead to the immediate guarantee of the Northern Bengal Railway, the Simla Railway, and other lines. The electric telegraph communication has been already productive of the most beneficial influence, in giving increased efficiency to military movements and the energetic action of the Government.

---

[54] Subathu.

1857 altered the British perspective on India in more ways than one.[55] With the shift from the East India Company, through the Government of India Act in 1858, there was a questioning of the nature and form of British rule, such as in the deliberations of the 1858 Parliamentary Commission on 'Colonization and Settlement of India'. The Hyde Clarke idea was partly one of governing the country from hill stations like Darjeeling and Shimla—'English towns', away from mainstream India. 'The railways provided a technological form that would sustain the power of these lineages. They would allow the British middle classes in India to preserve their distinct qualities by making it possible for them to travel throughout the territory and climate of India without being affected by it. They would also make it easy for them to travel to hill stations to recuperate their productive powers. In addition the railways would be run on the template of this moral and racial calculus of productivity.'[56] This explains the intent to add branch lines to trunk lines and the connecting of hill stations like Darjeeling, Shimla and places in the Nilgiris like Ooty. It also explains the focus on recruiting Eurasians at the subordinate levels of the railway bureaucracy. The trunk lines had enhanced the importance of the Madras, Calcutta and Bombay Presidencies. As more railway companies were formed, there were new lines weaving together Sindh and Multan to Punjab, Delhi to Amritsar and, in the extreme south, Negapatnam to Trichinopoly, Madurai

---

[55] See, for example, *Lines of the Nation: Indian Railway Workers, Bureaucracy, and the Intimate Historical Self*, Laura Bear, Columbia University Press, 2007.

[56] Laura Bear, *ibid.*

and Tuticorin. The events of 1857 also adversely affected railway construction because of the dislocation of people that followed. When construction revived, the conscious racial segregation became manifest in several ways. The British segregated themselves, not only in cantonments, but also in railway colonies and hill stations. Urban spaces, such as civil lines, were designed with this objective in mind. Lord Canning had succeeded Lord Dalhousie as Governor General in 1856, and he consciously focused on railway architecture to make stations defensible against attacks, suitable for ready conversion into army fortifications or temporary housing during times of emergency.

The railway station in Lucknow (the line to Lucknow was built in 1862) is a good example of this.

> The railway station was located in a vast open garden called the Charbagh, which was contiguous to the cantonment. The site was thought to be 'commercially central and strategically good, with the Cantonments in its rear'. The rebellion had prompted the official decision to convert all railway stations in British India into military posts. This entailed considerable expenditure to redesign and fortify existing nonmilitary railway stations. The Lucknow railway station was conceived at the right historical moment to fulfill the decision admirably well. It included a fort, arsenal, and barracks, and extra accommodation for the evacuation of Christians in the event of another outbreak in the city.[57]

---

[57] *The Making of Colonial Lucknow*, *1856–1877*, Veena Talwar Oldenburg, Princeton Legacy Library, 1984.

Since its military function became primary, the railway station became a restricted area, and only passengers were allowed on platforms. This caused considerable discontent. A newspaper complained: 'At some stations it is customary to prevent travellers from approaching too near [the Station] and only when tickets are being distributed are they allowed to go near the Station.'[58] Though not precluded from the first or second class carriages, Indians found it difficult to travel on them as the ticket collectors treated Indian passengers badly.

Circa 1870, several links of the trunk routes were falling into place. GIPR connected Bombay to Nagpur and Bombay to Jabalpur. Meanwhile, the EIRC built the Howrah–Delhi line, via Allahabad. Once the EIR's Allahabad–Jabalpur line (1867) and the GIPR's Mumbai–Jabalpur (1870) were done, the Howrah–Allahabad–Mumbai line could be opened up in 1870. In *Around the World in Eighty Days,* published in 1873, Phileas Fogg reaches Bombay ahead of schedule and buys a ticket from Bombay to Calcutta. However, despite what newspapers in London had reported, the conductor tells him, 'The railway isn't finished . . . The passengers know that they must provide means of transportation for themselves from Kholby to Allahabad.' That's how Fogg ends up hiring an elephant. It isn't clear where Kholby was—the author probably intended to indicate a place somewhere near Satna. News of the Howrah–Allahabad–Bombay railway line being opened was important enough for it to have reached Jules Verne.

---

[58] *Ibid.*

   The Bengal Nagpur Railway (BNR) was established
in 1871, and it was afterwards that parts of what are now
Bengal, Orissa and Chhattisgarh got connected through
railway networks. One of the purposes behind setting
up the BNR was a shorter Howrah–Bombay route. The
maps that follow are self-explanatory.

   During the later period, that is, after 1929, two delightful
limericks were published in the BNR house magazine.[59]
The reference is to Treverdyn Rashleigh Wynne. He
was successively agent and chief engineer of the BNR
(1887–1905), member and president of the Railway Board
(1905–14) and managing director of the BNR (1914–15).

   There's a line called the Bengal-Nagpore
   Constructed in days of long yore
   By the worthy Sir Trev'
   Who made the wheels rev'
   Till it earned every month half a crore.

That was the first limerick, referring to Wynne's early
association with the BNR. The second refers to his
later association with the company:

   There's a line called the Bengal-Nagpore.
   Which has suffered sad losses galore.
   Yet a 'Carroll' it sings
   For each cold weather brings
   A great 'Wynne' to the Railways once more.

---

[59] Quoted in, *South Eastern Railway, March To New Millennium*,
R.R. Bhandari, South Eastern Railway, 2001.

In a manner of speaking, Orissa was initially caught between two stools, fragmented between the British (Bengal) Presidency, the Madras Presidency and the Central Provinces. The Utkal Sabha, formally established in 1882, though it started functioning in the 1870s itself, played a fairly important role in articulating the demand for railway networks in Orissa. Though there were studies, such as for the Bankura–Midnapur and Balasore–Puri links, nothing very much happened until the Famine Commission Report of 1880. Rather oddly, though the earlier Bengal Orissa Famine Commission Report of 1867 had flagged the importance of roads, ports and canals, it hadn't thought railways were that important.[60] Railway development in Orissa had to wait till the 1890s. It wasn't just about Orissa. The Howrah–Allahabad–Bombay line traversed a very great distance, and now a Howrah–Nagpur–Bombay line, covering a distance of 1968 km, was being contemplated. In bits and pieces, this was eventually completed in 1900, thanks partly to the Bengal Nagpur Railway (BNR). Oddly, one had to wait for the BNR that came up in 1871 before parts of modern-day West Bengal, Odisha and Chhattisgarh got connected through railway networks.

One of the purposes behind setting up the BNR was to establish a shorter Howrah–Bombay route. On a map,

---

[60] See, for example, 'Development of Railway Transport in Colonial Orissa (1854–1936)', Ganeswar Nayak, *Orissa Review*, January 2008.

this looks closer to a straight line—at least, the Nagpur–
Bombay segment does. But the Howrah–Nagpur–
Bombay route is not as short as it initially appears to
be. A shorter Howrah–Bombay route ought to be via
Jabalpur. While there exists a Bombay–Jabalpur link, a
Jabalpur–Howrah link, cutting across Chhattisgarh and
Jharkhand, doesn't exist. If there was such a line, the
distance between Howrah and Bombay would be less
today. Some say it would be reduced by 400 km, others
say by 500 km. One guesses this depends on the precise
layout of the line.

The strange bit is that the British first seemed to have
thought of the Barwadih–Chirimiri link in 1925. That's
some ninety years ago. Chhattisgarh and Jharkhand are
mineral-rich, and were known to be so ninety years ago
too. The British wanted the link so that the coal reserves in
these areas could be exploited. Barwadih is in Jharkhand
and Chirimiri in Chhattisgarh. The distance between the
two stations is 182 km. Note that both the Barwadih and
the Chirimiri railway stations are connected by broad
gauge lines, but not to each other. There is some stuff
that is apocryphal but now elevated to railway legend.
Since this history hasn't been chronicled that well,
unlike that of major railway networks, you don't really
know what is true and what is not. Railway legend has
it that the British did a survey for Barwadih–Chirimiri,
acquired land for it and even started construction in
1930. Then World War II happened, and that was that.
Nothing happened for a long time, until the line was
officially approved in 1999.

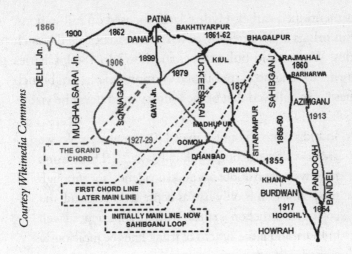

EIRC timeline

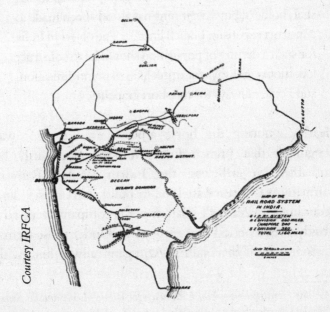

GIPR lines

As mentioned earlier, Hyde Clarke focused on hill stations. This brings in the question of what came to be called branch lines. Who would build these, and how? In 1860, Charles Burn, an engineer, published a monograph on branch lines.[61] He believed that branch lines would never be viable.

> In India, with a population of 110 per square mile, we are now constructing trunk railways . . . These trunk railways will no doubt pay good dividends, for although the population is only half as dense as in England, the cost of construction is small. We have commenced well in India, and if the system of trunk lines be judiciously carried out, they must prove most remunerative, and will no doubt become valuable property to the shareholders; but a beginning has already been made to construct expensive branch lines . . . The object in India for such a density of population should be to construct locomotive railways for trunk lines of communication, and horse railways for the short branches.

Clearly (ignoring the horse aspect), even then it was recognized that branch lines wouldn't necessarily be profitable. Nevertheless, the Indian Branch Railway Company was formed in 1862 to build short branch and feeder lines. Instead of a guarantee, the company received a subsidy over a period of twenty years. Under those terms, in 1863, it built the Nalhati–Azimganj railway line, with

---

[61] *On the Construction of Horse Railways for Branch Lines and for Street Traffic*, Charles Burn, John Weale, London, 1860.

a gauge (1222 mm) that was different from all the other gauges in existence then. Since the line never proved to be viable, it was taken over by the government in 1872. In 1866, the Indian Branch Railway Company started a metre gauge Lucknow–Kanpur line, under the twenty-year-subsidy terms. Though those terms were later altered to fit the old guarantee system prevalent then, this still didn't ensure success for the Indian Branch Railway Company. In 1872, it became part of the Oudh and Rohilkhand Railway.

The Indian Branch Railway Company left a legacy for Independent India. In November 2014, the ministry of railways issued sectoral guidelines for domestic and foreign private investments in railways, and this included renovation, operation and maintenance of standalone passenger corridors like branch lines and hill railways. This presupposes a definition of 'branch lines'. The (2013–14) Indian Railways Year Book stated:[62]

> Despite concerted efforts to enhance earnings on branch lines, most of these lines remain commercially unviable. The Railway Reforms Committee recommended closure of 40 such lines but due to stiff public resistance and opposition by state governments towards withdrawal of such services, only 15 lines have been closed permanently by the Railways. A review of the financial results of the existing 90 uneconomic branch lines for the year 2013-14 shows that, on an original investment

---

[62] *Indian Railways Year Book 2013–14*, Ministry of Railways and Railway Board.

on these lines of the order of Rs 2,617 crore, loss during
the year 2013-14 amounted to Rs 1,681 crore.

Branch lines, as it can be intuitively understood, are feeders.
But that still doesn't answer the question of a precise
definition. In 1969, there was a railway committee on
uneconomic branch lines, and there emerged some kind of
definition of 'branch line' as narrow gauge lines and those
broad and metre-gauge lines that join the main network
only at one end. There was also a kind of double definition
of an uneconomic or unremunerative branch line: (a) it did
not make profits; (b) it did not make profits more than the
rate of dividend paid to the Union government. Note that if
there is gauge conversion and switch from narrow to broad
gauge, the number of branch lines (and uneconomic lines)
declines. This doesn't mean those lines have been closed.
The Railway Reforms Committee that recommended
closure of forty branch lines is one that goes back to 1983.
At the turn of the century, there were 110 uneconomic
branch lines—forty-four broad-gauge, forty-four metre-
gauge and twenty-two narrow-gauge lines. According to the
2013–14 observation, the number is now down to ninety
(actually eighty-nine). Once upon a time, Indian Railways
had classified routes as mainline, suburban and branch line.
But that classification was scrapped in 1976, and based on
multiple criteria, broad gauge routes are now classified as
A, B, C, D and E, and metre gauge routes as Q, R and S.
A branch line can thus be interpreted as narrow gauge,
metre gauge or D and E categories of broad gauge lines, and
uneconomic branch lines as sub-categories of these. The

fact that we continue to use the expression 'branch line' is because we can't seem to get rid of the colonial legacy.

To return to history, in 1902, Lord Curzon went on a visit to the area around Lumding and had a conversation with the agent of the newly constructed railway line.[63]

'Now, Mr Woods, that you have built this line, what traffic do you expect to carry?'

'Nothing, sir.'

'Then why build the line at all?'

'I do not know,' was the reply. 'The Government of India ordered it to be built, sir!'

That's how many branch lines were built. 'The question of light railways on the narrow gauge arose as far back, at any rate, as 1862, when Mr J.E.Wilson (Agent for the Indian Branch Railway Company) informed the Government of India that he was "prepared to enter into definite arrangements for the construction of the roadways and the laying down of light railways thereon" in Oudh and Rohilkhand. In reply, the Government of India, while insisting upon the adoption of the 5 ft. 6 in. gauge for all railways intended to form portions of main lines, would sanction as a temporary expedient the construction of narrow-gauge light lines where the probable traffic was not sufficient to warrant a larger outlay, but only with the view of bringing them up to the standard in gauge and quality, when the traffic had so far developed as to require it. The Indian Branch Railway Company deserves particular mention,

---

[63] From the archived material at the National Academy of Indian Railways in Vadodara.

because, as Mr Horace Bell observes, "of all the numerous companies that were projected for building light railways in India, this was the only one in Northern India that actually did proceed to build lines." This Company laid a light railway of 4 ft. gauge on the public road from Azimganj to Nalhati in Bengal, but the line, after being bought by the Government of India, was relaid on the 5 ft. 6 in. gauge. Lord Canning was very much in favour of Mr Wilson's proposals for laying light narrow-gauge lines on existing roads as feeders to the standard-gauge trunk lines. Lord Elgin, however, insisted that the proposed light lines should be constructed on the 5 ft. 6 in. gauge, and Mr Wilson was not unready to accept this decision . . . It was well understood that in England engines of one company are rarely run on the line of another, and that the practical working of the railways is not compatible with such a system of interchange of engines, and that all that is ever requisite is the interchange of wagons and carriages . . . As soon as the Government gives up the system of guarantee, and abandons all right or desire to interfere in the management of railway companies' affairs, it ceases to be in a position to decide whether such a line shall be constructed of rails of one class or another.'

This was authored in 1899 by William Henry Cole and is reminiscent of some of the gauge conversion problems encountered much later.[64]

That giving up of the guarantee system takes us into the next chapter.

---

[64] *Light Railways at Home and Abroad*, William Henry Cole, C. Griffin & Company, 1899.

4

THE 1870S AND AFTER: CHANGE AND CONSOLIDATION

We will begin this chapter with the correspondence between 'P' and 'C' that appeared in the *Madras Times* of 1857.[65] Though the issue of railways versus irrigation had already been settled, and this 1857 correspondence chronologically belongs in the preceding chapter, we have included it here because it has a bearing on the profitability of the railways and the guarantee system. Neither P nor C revealed who they were. All that we know is that P was in favour of the railways and C argued against them, not only revisiting the railways-versus-irrigation debate, but also highlighting the fiscal burden that would result because of the railways. Though the jargon used today may be different, and there has been a shift from privately funded railway development to

---

[65] Compiled by the authors from Indian Railway archives.

publicly funded railway development, some issues are perennial. First, what is a reasonable rate of return on railway projects (meaning railway lines)? Second, not every railway project can be viable in a commercial sense. What does one do about positive externalities? Third, since there are opportunity costs of resources, how does one prioritize public expenditure on railways relative to expenditure on something else? (Though the following issues did not figure in the P-versus-C correspondence, we are flagging them.) Fourth, to what extent is railway development a natural monopoly? Can it be unbundled and some degree of choice and competition brought in? Fifth, to ensure fair rules of competition, what should be the role of a regulator? While we debate them today, it is remarkable that some of these issues were also debated, using different jargon, in the nineteenth century.

C, 1 January 1857:

P goes on to say, 'You argue from present traffic, from a traffic due to the most defective communication in the whole civilized world.' In the first place how are we to judge of communications, as to which are most defective; surely as in everything else by actual results. This is the only decisive test. At this moment there is a fair trial as to efficiency, between two kinds of communications. Which are we to consider the most defective, the one that carries a small part of the whole traffic on a certain line, or that which carries by far the greater part? Hitherto after four years' trial, the common road, and 'that not a very good one', as the late Consulting Engineer called it, has most decidedly beaten the Railway, and we must therefore conclude that there is one kind of communication more defective than a bad common road. The late Consulting Engineer truly said, 'The Railway cannot supersede the road in everything, not only so but if it cannot convey everything much cheaper than could be done by the road it must be pronounced a failure.' As far as any benefits can be expected from it in carrying the raw produce of the country, the Railway has actually thus failed after a four years' trial. But further, in our remarks was there one word about present traffic on the common roads? Every calculation was based upon the traffic on the Railways and that after from two to five years' working. We are at a loss to understand how P could charge us with arguing from present traffic on common roads. We argued solely from actual results on Railways opened sufficiently long, and to a sufficient length to afford a very considerable data as to how far they would operate in the creation of traffic. P next observes that the work of the Railway is to convey men and goods cheaper, safer, and faster, than they have ever yet been carried. Did P really write this seriously? Is he really not aware that water carriage is cheaper than that by Railway? What are we to think of that side of a discussion which leads men to make such strange assertions? On the Hudson River in New York, 1st class passengers are carried at from 16 to 18 miles an hour at 2 ½ pence a mile, allowing for the difference in the value of money, much less than ½ pence, in India. P then proceeds gravely to remonstrate with us on our

endeavours to show from actual results on the four most
important lines of communication in India, the entire
failure of the Railways, both as a speculation and as
providing the first grand desideratum for a poor country,
cheap transit. He says, 'Let me remind you that you take
upon yourself no small responsibility in attempting to
render unpopular and discourage these great works.'
One might be excused smiling on reading this. Is there
no responsibility in labouring to keep up this delusion in
spite of the facts which the last five years have produced?
No responsibility in stating that Railways carry cheaper
than any other means? He then goes on to speak of the
'effects of those great works on the country, in carrying
produce three or four times cheaper than at present and
in the introduction of European skill and capital among
them'.

C, 10 January 1857:

We refer again to P's grave warnings respecting our
responsibility in trying thoroughly to examine this
question, and of the danger of our remarks discouraging
British enterprise in India. We would only ask, which is
most likely to check the introduction of British Capital
into India, those leading men into an expenditure of many
millions upon works which certainly cannot possibly pay
even bare interest, or those warning them against such,
and pointing out to them those that being really suited
to the circumstances and wants of the country, will
probably yield abundant returns. Let us suppose that

instead of nominal net profits of 2 and 4 per cent, such as the Railways are now paying after the expenditure has been going on for six or eight years, the subject had been submitted to real discussion, and in consequence, the same money had been expended on works yielding 20 or 30 per cent, in how different a position would we now have been with respect to the introduction of British Capital into India? The effects of the Railways in this respect have only been to make people in England suppose that Indian investments are hopeless things. So that at this moment only a trifling amount of Capital, excepting what is forced in by the guarantee, has yet been invested here. The prodigious profits on River Navigation have indeed now at length begun to convince the people at home, that there is at least one opening for profitable investment, and no doubt this will help to counteract the ruinous effects of the Railway speculation. But if only a small portion of the millions already spent upon the Railways, and the six or eight years employed upon them, had been applied to highly productive water works, long before this, British Capital would have poured into India abundantly without guarantee. P writes as if the whole question lay between Railways and Roads; one would suppose from reading only his letter, that there were no such things as Rivers and Canals. The real question is, shall we make use of our immense natural advantage in our magnificent rivers, both for Navigation themselves and to supply Canals, or shall we madly continuing to throw away these great gifts, persist in purchasing communications that will not answer our main purpose at all, at a cost of one or two lacs per mile, works that will neither carry cheap nor yield returns?

P, 19 January 1857:

Sir, I now proceed to consider the continuation of your article on Indian Railways as given in the paper of the 10th instant. I find in this fallacies and one-sided arguments which have been exposed and refuted over and over again. But the village schoolmaster of Goldsmith was no mere whimsical emanation from the poet's brain—he was the type and representative of a large class in every generation—'though vanquished they will argue still'; and these fallacies and their so-called arguments must still be met and still be refuted; for uttered as they are with dogmatic tone and shrouded in a mist of so-called calculations that render the subject wholly unintelligible to the multitude, they produce their effect 'non vi sed sape cadendo'. There are two or three indisputable facts which I wish to impress upon your mind, since you appear either to be wholly unaware of them or to have entirely overlooked them. 1st. The working expenses per ton mile, or per passenger mile necessarily fall as the amount of traffic increases, and the very small amount of expense necessarily due to the movement of a passenger is illustrated by very careful calculations made in Belgium from actual results, which showed that the portion of that expense which was not susceptible of continued reduction as the amount of traffic increased, was only the 1/200th part of a penny per passenger mile. 2nd. The working expenses are obviously greater on a short length of line than on a longer one, especially in the cost of management in each department. 3rd. It is a mischievous and oft exposed fallacy to speak of a railway as if it were a luxury for a rich people and a rich country. You compare it, as I have heard it done before by men who had not had the means or the inclination to study the subject, to a 'State carriage and four'. The analogy is utterly unsound. A State carriage and four could not carry bags of rice so cheaply as a bandy and pair of bullocks. The Railway can and does do it cheaper. Have you been in Europe during these last thirty years or have you been there to no purpose? Have you never seen or heard of a hundred thousand Pounds being invested in building Steam Engines to make the cloth that is intended to enfold the loins of the poorest among men? Do you not know that for years past, the application of Capital to the manufacture of the commonest article of consumption has been cheapening these articles, and driving from their looms thousands of the industrious poor, and are we expected now to believe in the year of Grace 1857, that steam power is a luxury for the rich, a discovery with which the poor have no concern? It is some years now since a popular and intelligent Officer of Cavalry, now gone, said with a good-natured though rather contemptuous smile, 'No, no, you can't carry bratties by railway yet.' I replied 'why not,' to which there was no answer. He remembered perhaps, though you have forgotten, the old nursery problem, of the difference between a pound of lead and a pound of feathers, and it may have flashed across his clear and unbiased mind, that if a railway could carry a ton of beer cheaper than a bullock cart could it must also beat the latter in the conveyance of a ton of bratties; and let it not be forgotten, that the lines which pay the best are those chiefly occupied with coal and other mineral traffic. So let us hear no more if you please of your carriage and four.

C, 28 March 1857:

We have written so much lately against Railways in general in India, that we hope we may be allowed for a change to offer something in favour of a Railway in particular in this country. We cannot see the use of trying to persuade ourselves that a thing is what we know it is not. How much better to open our eyes to the actual and palpable state of the case and then consider what, under these circumstances, we had better do. The present gross receipts of the first 120 miles of the Madras Railway, and excluding Railway materials, are under 100 Rs a week per mile, or 5000 Rs a year, and if we take 40 per cent of this for the present excess of receipts over disbursements and 80,000 Rs a mile as the Capital, the nominal profits are 2 per cent, without any allowance for heavy repairs or depredation. At Vellore the Railway loses all the North West traffic, and at Vaniembaddy all the Western traffic. It is quite certain that the South West traffic, which is all that will pass along the Railway beyond Vaniembaddy, will not exceed 1/6th of the whole, so that for the next 300 miles, the traffic will be quite insignificant and even in the last 100 miles, adjoining the Western Coast, it is quite certain that the traffic cannot be a quarter of what it is at this end, on the part entering the Capital. Probably Beypoor and Calicut don't contain more than one-twentieth part of the population of Madras, and not one-hundredth part of its wealth. Nothing therefore but the most wilful shutting of our eyes to plain facts can hinder us from seeing that the Railway cannot pay its interest; nay much more; as the nominal profits in this productive part are 2 per cent which is, so far as we have data, about the amount of depreciation, it seems certain that the whole line will not nearly pay its expenses, so that there seems no ground at all for hope that it will remain in the hands of the Company, the Shareholders will receive their 5 per cent, for the terms of the guarantee do not secure them in this, unless the Railway pays its expenses. It seems evident that the Directors and Shareholders have begun to consider this point, for at the last Shareholders' meeting the chairman said that at the next they could insist upon the Government taking this concern off their hands. For their own sakes the sooner the Shareholders get this arrangement made, the better. It only remains for us now to look this disappointment in the face like men, and consider what is best to be done under the circumstances. The money has been sunk, and the question now should be simply, how we can make the best of the case. Can we not get any return for our money; is there no use to which the Railway can be applied so as to save the country from a tremendous loss? Happily the moment we turn our eyes from a delusion to the realities of the case, the value of the Work is as obvious as its failure in respect of the objects originally aimed at.

The next bit of correspondence is not from Madras, but from London. On 26 October 1861, W.P. Andrew, Chairman of the Scinde Railway Company, wrote a letter to the *Times,* London. He said,

> Sir, Attempts are being made by ignorant or interested persons to misrepresent the nature of the guarantee or other privileges granted to Indian railways, and, as I have been a party to no less than three of the contracts with the Secretary of State for India in Council conferring, those advantages, the favor of your allowing me to give, in as few words as possible, what I believe is accepted both by Government on the one hand and the companies on the other, as the intent and meaning of the reciprocal engagements entered into. The guarantee of a minimum rate of interest on the capital is for 99 years, with lease of the land necessary for the railway and works for a like period free of charge. On the opening of a Line all net profits exceeding the rate of interest guaranteed are to be divided; one-half of the surplus is to go to the Shareholders, and the other half to the Government, in liquidation of the interest they have advanced. When the interest advanced by Government has been repaid, the entire surplus profit goes to the Shareholders. The Government reserve a right to regulate the trains and fares, and, as

soon as the dividend exceeds ten per cent, to lower
the fares, but not so as to reduce the profit below that
rate. The Government also reserve power, after the
first twenty-five or fifty years, to purchase a Line at a
price equal to the average market value of its shares
for the three preceding years. On the other hand, a
Railway Company has the power at any time, after
a line or any portion of it has been three months in
work, to require the Government to take it off their
hands at six months' notice and repay them the whole
of the capital expended. The contract of the Indus
Steam Flotilla is as similar to that of the Railways
as circumstances admitted, due provision being
made out of profits for the renewal and insurance
of the vessels. The Companies cannot borrow on
mortgage, but the debentures of the Railways and
the Indus Steam Flotilla have these words on the
face of each bond: 'Payment of principal and interest
is guaranteed by the Secretary of State for India in
Council, and this is authenticated by the signature
of the Under Secretary of State. The guarantee of
the Indian Government is only second to that of
the Imperial Government. Its security rests on the
revenues of India; but to preserve them, as you lately
remarked, the whole force of the empire would be
used. When we lose India it would be high time for
the fund holder to put his house in order.' It is very
easy to find fault with any arrangement, but I should
like those who would attempt to decry the liberal
terms and conditions granted to Indian Railways

and the Indus Steam Flotilla to point out any Government guarantee so advantageous as the one in question. The several contracts of this Company with Government, and the Acts of Parliament of the Company, are open at this office for the inspection of those who are desirous of more detailed information. I am Sir, your most obedient servant.

In response, on 1 November 1861, James Mills wrote a letter to the newspaper:

Sir, I invite you to publish the following correspondence: I lately put forth a pamphlet calling attention to the real nature of the Indian Guarantees. This pamphlet appears to have excited some attention, and at a late Meeting of the Scinde Railway and Indus Flotilla Companies, the Chairman, Mr W.P. Andrew referred to it in slighting terms, and maintained the opposite of the doctrines I had propounded. In a Second Edition I replied to Mr Andrew, vindicating the views I had formerly expressed, and as my arguments appear to have been considered of weight in some quarters, a letter appeared from Mr Andrew in the Money Article of the *Times* of October 26th reciting the main conditions of the contract with the Government; and the topics I raised were also touched upon by the Chairmen of the East Indian and Indian Peninsula Railways at the recent Meetings of Proprietors, and have also been discussed with considerable ability

by Mr Thomas Watt, the Secretary of the Indian
Peninsula Railway, in a pamphlet he has lately
published. To all this I can see no objection. My
views, if they can be shown to be wrong, ought to
be confuted. But in most of the main points, this
confutation has yet to be given, and whatever may
be thought of the strength of my positions, public
opinion will be at least unanimous in the conviction
that such questions can only be investigated by the
aid of dispassionate discussion, and are not to be
resolved by the bludgeon process of a legal threat.
The letter which I forwarded to the *Times* in reply to
that of Mr Andrew, was not inserted. Intimidation
I am informed has been used towards the publisher
of my pamphlet, to frighten him against continuing
the sale, and now the same species of illegitimate
pressure is sought to be put upon myself, with what
result the subjoined correspondence will show.
To what end all these attempts at suppression, if
my views are so superficial and my arguments
so destitute of weight as is pretended? When Mr
Andrew is able to show that his Indus Flotilla
Guarantees, which, on the strength of receiving
5 per cent *from*, undertakes to pay 17 per cent *to
the* Government, is a species of security, which, in
common with a loan, will return at least 5 per cent
interest to the investor under all contingencies,
there may be some reason in seeking to attract the
public attention to the nature of the guarantee given
to this concern. But until he can perform this feat,

the more he stirs the matter the worse must be the impression conveyed. I am, Sir, Your obedient Servant.

With this letter to the *Times*, dated 1 November 1861, James Mills attached some correspondence, initiated by a letter he had received from Mr Andrew on 31 October 1861: 'Mr James Mills, Sir, As I have been unable to meet with you, I have to ask you to do one of two things, either give me up the name of the real author of the Pamphlet on Indian Railway and Flotilla Guarantees published by Messrs' Mann Nephews, 39, Cornhill, London, or sign the enclosed note for publication.' The enclosed note said:

Sir, I much regret having been misled into making false statements in the pamphlet, on Indian Guarantees, published by Messrs' Mann Nephews, 39, Cornhill. The further publication of the Pamphlet has been suppressed, and I hereby tender you my humble and sincere apology.' James Mills's response to W.P. Andrew, dated 31 October 1861, was, 'Sir, I am greatly astonished at the unwarrantable liberty you have taken in addressing to me such a letter, and submitting to me such a proposal as I have just received from you. I presume I am at liberty to discuss any public question without asking your permission, and if you endeavour as you have publicly done, to controvert my views, I have yet to learn that it is not permissible in me to return such a reply to your criticisms as I am able to give. If in the heat of argument I have used any word or phrase which might be considered to be characterized by needless asperity, I should have been quite willing to rectify it on proper application having been made to me, and am still willing to do so in my next edition if such words are pointed out. But I am not to be moved by intimidation. You will find it as difficult to silence me by threats as you appear to have found it to silence me by argument, and I am quite astonished that such an attempt should be made by any one claiming the least title to self-respect. As it will suffice to show the public what influences are at work to stifle inquiries into the pretensions of these guarantees, I propose to publish your letter, and this answer to it, and I have directed my solicitors, Messrs' Cotterill and Sons, Throgmorton Street to attend to any further communications which you may wish to address to me, being quite prepared to defend whatever I have written.'

On 4 November 1861, W.P. Andrew wrote to James Mills, 'It was natural for your contemptible employer to be insolent at the moment he claims the protection of his solicitor. Be assured I will unearth and punish you both before I have done with you.' It is a great pity that we don't know what happened of this affair later. In all probability, nothing very much happened, since James Mills reprinted the pamphlet and subsequent editions included this entire correspondence.[66]

---

[66] *Indian Railway and Indus Flotilla Guarantees Examined and Found to be Delusive*, James Mills, Wilson & Company, London, 3rd edition 1861.

The problems with this old guarantee system have been mentioned earlier. Net earnings were paid into the treasury and rebated to the company. If the net earnings fell short of the guaranteed return of 5 per cent, the government bore the difference. This was treated as debt. If net earnings were more than the guaranteed return of 5 per cent, any surplus profits were transferred to the government, and this was regarded as repayment of the past guarantee payments or debt. Once all such guarantees had been paid off, the company received the entire amount of surplus profits. This was the crux, although there were other issues, like the way foreign exchange exposure was treated.[67] Those guarantees were expensive for the government, especially when construction costs were high and profits low. There was no incentive for companies to reduce costs and capital expenditure. The simple view is that the guarantee system changed in 1869. Indeed, as a thumbnail sketch, one could think of four phases of railway construction in India: (1) the phase up to 1869, with private companies constructing lines (particularly trunk routes) under this old guarantee system; (2) the government of India entering construction and managing the railways, a phase that lasted throughout the 1870s; (3) hybrid public-private partnerships from the early 1880s, with the government of India owning most of the lines and

---

[67] See, for example, 'Railways in Colonial India: An Economic Achievement?' Dan Bogart and Latika Chaudhary, May 2012, www.ssrn.com/abstract=2073256.

private companies involved in their construction and operations; (4) the government of India taking over railway operations, starting in 1924.[68] Within that fourth phase, some changes came in when the Railway Board was introduced in 1905.

The opening of Burdwan station of the EIRC in 1855

Courtesy National Rail Museum, Delhi

This simple thumbnail sketch serves a purpose, but one must remember that life was much more complicated. Towards the close of the nineteenth century, there were ten different railway systems, in simultaneous existence: (1) Lines constructed, owned and operated by private companies under old contracts and guarantees; (2) Lines constructed, owned and operated by private companies under new contracts and guarantees; (3) Lines constructed, owned and operated by the government of India; (4) Lines owned by the government of India, but

---

[68] *Ibid.*

constructed and operated by private companies; (5) Lines constructed and operated by private companies, without a guarantee, but with some kind of government assistance; (6) Lines owned and operated by the princely states; (7) Lines owned by the princely states, but operated by the government; (8) Lines owned by princely states, but operated by private companies; (9) District board lines, short local lines within a district, financed through a local cess; and (10) Lines in foreign (French or Portuguese territory). 'By 1902, the intricate combinations of ownership and management had led to a railway network which was operated by 33 separate administrations, which included 24 private companies, 4 government agencies and five princely states.'[69]

The chronology of the evolution of this system is shown in Table 1.[70] Since the expressions 'productive line' and 'protective line' are used in the table, it is necessary to clarify what they mean, though the answer is obvious enough. Productive lines had commercial importance, with the potential to generate returns. They could therefore be built by private companies. Protective lines were those with limited commercial importance, and were therefore unlikely to be financially viable and also unlikely to be constructed through the raising of loans.

---

[69] Introduction in Roopa Srinivasan, Manish Tiwari and Sandeep Silas, *op. cit.*
[70] Collated on the basis of Sanyal, *op. cit,* and the IRFCA website.

Table 1: Evolution of Policies and Committees, 1850–1947

Year	Policies/ Committees	Nature of Contract/ Administration/ Recommendations	Railway Companies & Lines
1849	Guarantee System	Any company that constructed railways was guaranteed 5% rate of interest on its capital investment The Government retained the power, after 25 or 50 years, of purchasing the railway Land was to be provided free by the State for the railways Policy of short experimental lines **Supervision and administration** a) Central government b) Consulting engineer of guaranteed railways c) Provincial consulting engineer carried out the routine work, inspection of lines etc. **Government:** Alignment, position and arrangements of the stations	**Companies** East India Railway Company Great Indian Peninsula Railway **Lines** Short experimental lines were undertaken

Year	Policies/ Committees	Nature of Contract/ Administration/ Recommendations	Railway Companies & Lines
1853	Undertaking Trunk Routes under Old Guarantee System	Policy of short experimental lines was given up To connect ports with the Presidencies, and the Presidencies (Bombay, Bengal and Madras) with each other	**Companies** Madras Railway Company Scinde Railway Company Bombay, Baroda and Central Railway Company Great Southern of India Railway Company **Lines** Calcutta to Delhi & North West Frontier Bombay to Delhi Madras towards West Coast
Late 1850s to 1868	*Attempts were made to form Unguaranteed companies as the Guarantee System was turning out to be burdensome. 1857 stressed the need for more rapid development*		
1858	Parliamentary Committee	To enquire into the cause for delays in constructing railways in India	

Year	Policies/ Committees	Nature of Contract/ Administration/ Recommendations	Railway Companies & Lines
1863 1866	Unguaranteed companies and lines	To construct short feeder lines on narrower gauge. No interference of government except assistance in terms of granting land, undertaking surveys	**Companies** Indian Branch Railway Company Indian Tramway Company **Lines** Nalhati to Azimganj Aroconum to Kancheepuram 1865—Delhi and Agra to Jaipore
1867	*The policy of un-guaranteeing the companies and railway lines failed and the companies resorted to the Guarantee System. The companies failed to attract any investors. Thus the new contracts were under modified terms.*		
1869 1870	State construction and management	The State carried on construction and management under its own agency Financial responsibility on the government Metre gauge adopted	**Princely or Native State Railways** Nizam State Railways Holkar Railway

Year	Policies/ Committees	Nature of Contract/ Administration/ Recommendations	Railway Companies & Lines
		Distinction between productive and protective railway lines made	Tirhoot State Railway
			Mysore State Railway
		Princely or Native railway lines were encouraged	Rajputana State Railway
1874		**Management and Administration**	**Railway Companies**
1877		Enhanced the Central government's power	1874—South India Railway Company
		Post of consulting engineer for State Railways constituted	1878—Nagpur Chhattisgarh Railway
		Provincial consulting engineers to supervise the new state lines and the guaranteed railways within their jurisdiction.	1888—Bengal Nagpur Railway
1879			
1882		A deputy controller for each line made responsible for the accounts and financial management	
		The engineers and the controllers were directly under the orders of the government which acted on the advice of the consulting engineer for state railways and of the Accountant-General	

Year	Policies/ Committees	Nature of Contract/ Administration/ Recommendations	Railway Companies & Lines
		1874—State Railway Directorate formed	
		1877—State Railways divided into three systems a) Central, comprising Rajputana, Holkar, Scindia, and Neemuch Railways; b) Western, including Indus-Valley, and the Punjab-Northern line: and c) North-Eastern, covering the state lines under direct control in Bengal and Assam.	
		Government control and supervision of the guaranteed railways continued to be exercised through local consulting engineers	
		1879—The EIR purchased	
		1881–82 Railways of India classified into a) Guaranteed Railways b) State Railways	
		New Companies formed known as	
		c) Assisted Companies	
		State Railways further classified under	
		a) Imperial state b) Provisional state c) Native state Railways	

Year	Policies/ Committees	Nature of Contract/ Administration/ Recommendations	Railway Companies & Lines
1880s to 1902	*Attempts made to revive Companies*		
1880	Finance Commission	Recommended 20,000 miles of railway lines for protective purposes and an immediate addition of not less than 5000 miles.	
1880s 1881 1882	Revival of Companies	Adoption of a policy of allowing 'safe and reasonable guarantees' to attract private enterprise for railway construction The companies were left free in the management and working of the lines The government reserved the right of purchase or ultimate lapse to the state, and such powers of supervision and control of rates and fares as would safeguard the interests of the public Further, the advances for interest made, if any, during construction, were to be repaid out of surplus revenue in subsequent years.	**Companies** Bengal and Central Railway Rohilkhand–Kumaun–Southern Maratha Bengal and North Western Railway

Year	Policies/ Committees	Nature of Contract/ Administration/ Recommendations	Railway Companies & Lines
1884	Parliamentary Select Committee	Distinction between protective and productive line was given up	**Companies** Indian Midland Railway Company
1885 1887 1892		Favoured extension of the railways for Protection of famines Promotion of internal and external trade Opening of fertile tracts and coalfields	Bengal Nagpore Company Assam Bengal Railway Company
		Both state and private enterprise promoted as agency	
		A sum of £500,000 was permitted to be spent on 'protective' or non-productive lines out of borrowed money over and above the usual grant from the Famine Reserve Fund and from revenues.	
		Entrusting of the management of various Indian state lines to English-guaranteed companies either newly formed, or already in existence in adjoining British territories	

Year	Policies/ Committees	Nature of Contract/ Administration/ Recommendations	Railway Companies & Lines
1893	Branch Lines *The 1893 proposal was revised thrice. Once in 1896, the second time in 1910 and the third time in 1914.*	The 1893 proposal was made after failing to attract private enterprise and capital (on a sterling basis)	**Railway lines:** South Behar line Tapti Valley
1896		Invited capital on a rupee basis for the construction of branch lines	Ahmedabad–Parantij **State ownership of railway lines**
		Land was to be given free, surveys being made at state expense	**1884**—Eastern Bengal Railway acquired by the government
		Branch lines were made by the main line administrations who should have a prior right to construct them	**1885**—The Scind Punjab and Delhi Railway acquired and incorporated with the Punjab –Northern and Indus–Valley state lines to form the North Western Railway system
1897		The gauge, route, moving dimensions, stations, etc. would be subject to the approval of government	
		Government reserved the usual rights of supervision, control of rates and fares, and of purchase at the end of 21years	**1889**—The Oudh and Rohilkhand Railway purchased.
			1890—The South Indian Railway acquired
		Management and Administration Post of Under-Secretary, an Assistant Secretary and Accountant General, PWD, created	**1900**—The Great Indian Peninsula Railway purchased

Year	Policies/ Committees	Nature of Contract/ Administration/ Recommendations	Railway Companies & Lines
		Post of Secretary, GOI, PWD, created Post of consulting engineer for state railways abolished	1900—The Indian Midland Railway which was working the Bhopal–Itarsi, Scindia State, Bina–Goona and Bhopal–Ujjain lines, in addition to the sections constructed by the company as agents of the state, was merged into the Great Indian Peninsula System
1905	Sir Thomas Robertson Committee Railway Board constituted	Among many recommendations, the Railway Board recommendation was implemented The function and powers of railways under the PWD were transferred to the Railway Board It comprised the following members: Chairman of the Board, a Railway Manager from England and an Agent of a Company Railway	

Year	Policies/ Committees	Nature of Contract/ Administration/ Recommendations	Railway Companies & Lines
1921	Acworth Committee	A unified management of the entire railway system was adopted. Government took over the management of railways Separated railway finances from general government finances **Reconstituted board:** Chief Commissioner, a Financial Commissioner and two Members— Member, Way and Works, Projects and Stores; and Member, General Administration, Staff and Traffic subjects.	
1922– 23 1924	Retrenchment Committee	Recommended drastic cuts in working expenses and other measures designed to produce a fixed annual profit for the state. Railway finances separated from general finances in the general government budget	

Year	Policies/ Committees	Nature of Contract/ Administration/ Recommendations	Railway Companies & Lines
1930s 1940s	World War II. Railways under strain again. Locomotives, wagons, and track material are taken from India to the Middle East. Railway workshops are used to manufacture shells and other military equipment. The entire railway system is in poor shape by the end of the War. Zonal regrouping of Railways done.		

Despite the complications, after some mergers, consolidation and renaming, the major companies in 1869 were East Indian; Great Indian Peninsula; Eastern Bengal; Bombay, Baroda and Central India; Sind, Punjab and Delhi; Madras; South Indian; and Oudh and Rohilkhand. What kind of a policy regime would these companies be subjected to? That was the primary question.

An illustration from *London News* of people waiting in the platform for the train, 1854

Courtesy IRFCA

There was no question of continuing the old guarantee system. Other than perverse incentives for the private companies, it was simply too expensive. In 1873, C.H.G. Jenkinson, assistant engineer of the Western Rajputana State Railway, wrote,

Ask why all the Indian Railways have on an average cost enormous sums, out of all proportions to the wealth of our country. They traverse on exceptionally plain country for the greater part of their length and the average of heavy works on them cannot be said to be exceptionally high. Is the reason this, that the proprietors of the lines and their servants have not sufficient interest in the country, and because the former, living in England and never thinking of their property, except to receive 5 per cent on it when it becomes due; the latter only of their pay, they contemplating only a short residence in the country, do not consult the best interest of the inhabitants for doing what the public servants of this country have ever been justly famed? This accusation is not to be denied, and no one can have travelled far in this country by railway without remarking the profuse liberality with which money has been spent, without the smallest regard to the wants of the country, or indeed to the habits of the natives. The Government therefore, has been wise to undertake the construction of new lines itself, and to entrust the work to men who look forward to a lengthened residence in India, and who can hardly help in a measure identifying themselves with the interests of the country they have adopted for the best years of their lives.[71]

Especially between 1864 and 1868, there was uproar against the old guarantee system.

---

[71] Quoted in, *South Eastern Railway, March to New Millennium*, R.R. Bhandari, South Eastern Railway, 2001.

Criticism of the old guarantee system should have led to its tweaking. It did not logically follow that the state would itself have to undertake the building of railways. Therefore, there was a broader debate too, even if it was not always articulated explicitly. That broader debate was about the role of private enterprise vis-à-vis the role of government, and that pendulum was gradually shifting towards the government.[72] This shift of the pendulum towards state provisioning was not an isolated Indian phenomenon.[73] When experiments with tweaking the old guarantees, such as with the Indian Branch Railway Company, didn't work, that was further grist to the mill for the pro-government side. Lord Lawrence was Governor General of India between 1864 and 1869, and Lord Mayo Governor General between 1869 and 1872. The watershed was a Minute by Lord Lawrence. This was dated 9 January 1869, three days before he was to demit office. It said, 'Is it reasonable or consistent with the true interests of India to continue a system under which the revenues have to bear the whole risk or loss and can derive no direct benefit from railway construction, in preference to one under which with a risk certainly no greater and probably much reduced, the whole of the direct profits can be added to the public revenues and made available for reducing taxation or preventing the imposition of

---

[72] See the compelling arguments in, *The Role of the State in the Provision of the Railways*, Mira Jagtiani, London, 1924. Interestingly, the introduction was written by William Acworth.

[73] *National Railways: An Argument for State Purchase*, James Hole, Cassel and Company, London, 1895 is an example.

new burdens?'[74] Lord Mayo, the successor, accepted the Minute and the shift. Hence, 1869 is generally regarded as signalling a shift in railway policy.

But the railway edifice was still a complicated structure. In some cases, as in the examples described below, there was outright state agency and state capital. There were other cases that happened a bit later, like the Tirhut Railway, in 1886.

(1) We have already encountered Indus Flotilla, the steamship company established in 1859. The Indus Flotilla Company was merged with Indus Valley State Railway, the latter being formed in 1879 under the state agency/state capital template. Indus Valley State Railway opened the Multan-Kotri line in 1878. Later, in 1886, Indus Valley State Railway would merge with Scinde Railway (formed in 1855), Punjab Railways, Delhi Railway and Punjab Northern State Railway to form North Western State Railway. However, in 1870, through some mergers, we already had the Scinde, Punjab and Delhi Railways, and there is something we should remember this railway company for. The government was concerned with overcrowding on railway platforms and only passengers were allowed on platforms. Those who accompanied passengers complained. Therefore, on 7 August 1883, the government of India addressed a letter to the Bombay government. This said,

---

[74] Quoted in Bhandari, *loc.cit.* Bhandari suggests that the Minute was actually authored by Richard Strachey.

At present, as a rule, only those natives who have railway tickets are admitted on to the platform, and it has been represented that considerable inconvenience is caused by the custom generally in force which prevents native gentlemen from being present on the platform to meet a friend or relative coming by train or to accompany him on his departure. The Government of India fully recognized the necessity of preventing the undue crowding of railway platforms, but it is thought that the grievance complained of might be to a great extent remedied, without inconvenience to railway working, by the adoption, at the principal stations, of a system lately introduced by the Sind, Punjab & Delhi Railway at Lahore of issuing platform tickets at a small charge which might be fixed experimentally at one or two pice for each ticket.[75]

This is how we learn that Scinde (Sind) Punjab and Delhi Railways were the first railways to introduce platform tickets, in Lahore. This wasn't the end of the matter, since it wasn't very clear that railway authorities could bar non-ticket holders (including those without platform tickets) from entering platforms. The matter was clarified through a government of India circular dated 20 December 1883: 'His Excellency, the Governor General is pleased to rule that, in future, when the Railway Authorities desire to exclude all but ticket holders from railway platforms, the intention shall be duly notified in the railway timetables,

---

[75] Railwaysofraj.blogspot.in

and a printed notice to that effect specifying the place where such tickets are obtainable and their cost, shall be drawn up with reference to Section 3 (C) and 41 of the Indian Railways Act No. IV of 1879 and pasted up in a conspicuous place outside the station.'[76]

(2) The Punjab Northern State Railway (1869) deserves special mention because it was the first railway that was set up with state agency and state capital. Lahore railway station had been opened in 1862 and the Amritsar–Lahore, Lahore–Multan, Amritsar–Delhi and Lahore–Karachi linking lines were made. Punjab Northern State Railway's main contribution were the Lahore–Peshawar and Lahore–Jhelum links.

(3) The Rajputana Malwa Railway was formed in 1876, though in its initial years it was known as the Rajputana State Railway. The name was changed in 1882. Its contribution consisted of the Delhi–Ajmer, Ajmer–Indore, Ajmer–Ahmedabad, Ajmer–Khandwa and Jodhpur–Marwar links. In 1889, the Bombay, Baroda and Central India Railway (BBCI) took over the management of the Rajputana Malwa Railway, and eventually merged it into itself in 1900. Building the railways wasn't only about building railway lines. One needed workshops too, like the Jamalpur workshop mentioned earlier. In 1876–77, the Rajputana Malwa Railway established a workshop in Ajmer for the manufacture of steam locomotives, carriages and wagons. The first indigenous locomotive,

[76] *Ibid.*

as opposed to imported ones, was built (it was actually assembled) in 1895 by the Ajmer Workshop (now part of North Western Railway). This was the metre gauge F1-734, 'F' signifying mixed traffic. The F1-734 was retired in the 1950s and is now housed at the National Rail Museum, cow-catcher and all. The Jamalpur Locomotive Workshop, set up by the East India Railway in 1862, followed in 1899 with the 'Lady Curzon', numbered CA-764. In those days, that locomotive cost Rs 33,000 to make. The Lady Curzon retired in 1932 and no one knows where this locomotive is now.

The F1-734 locomotive[77]

The expansion of the railway network was still not fast enough to deal with national developments. (The network of 4265 miles in 1869 had increased to only 6128 miles by 1879.) There was a serious famine in 1876–78, especially concentrated in the south and south-western parts of the country, at least in the beginning. The famine subsequently spread to the north and central parts of the country. Estimates

---

[77] Photograph courtesy Nigel Tout, www.nigeltout.com

are that this famine led to a direct death toll of 5.5 million, apart from the other ravages it caused. There were multiple reasons for the famine. It led to the setting up of the Famine Commission that submitted its report in 1880. This report led to a Draft Indian Famine Code, among other things. For our purposes, this report flagged the less-than-satisfactory expansion of the railway network in the country.

> There would be manifest advantages in giving free scope to the extension of railways by private enterprise if it were possible; and, though the original form of guarantee has been condemned, it may not be impossible to find some substitute which shall be free from its defects, and may secure the investment of capital in these undertakings without involving the Government in financial or other liabilities of an objectionable nature.[78]

After another cycle of famines in 1896–97, there was another Famine Commission Report in 1898. A quote from this report is interesting:[79]

> The public works programmes should also include such railway works as may be feasible, and should be prepared in communication with the officers of the Railway Department. The rules prescribed by the

---

[78] Quoted in Bhandari, *loc. cit.*
[79] *Report of the Indian Famine Commission of 1898*, reprinted by Agricole Publishing Company, Delhi, 1979.

Government of India regarding the inclusion of railway projects in the programme of relief works *are* sound, and require no modification. We understand, however, that an extensive railway construction programme is now maintained and annually reconsidered and revised in the Public Works Secretariat, and it may be possible to employ relief labour more extensively in future upon railway works which, though not finally sanctioned, may have been entered in these programmes. There may also often be minor works on railways to which those rules do not apply which would form useful relief works, such as the excavation of reservoirs at railway stations, diversions of road approaches when it is proposed to substitute an overhead for a level crossing, collection of ballast, etc. If some of these works though desirable are not worth the full normal cost, arrangements might be made here also for charging only a portion of their cost to the railway.

The Famine Commission Report of 1880 didn't think the railway construction programme was extensive enough. Against that baseline of 6128 miles in 1879, it wanted an expansion in the network to 20,000 miles. Of this, 5000 miles was to be done on an urgent basis. The network, in 1881, had expanded to 9875 miles, considered another benchmark.

Lines were constantly being built, as Table 2[80] shows. The Nagpur Chhattisgarh Railway (its first line opened in 1880), later merged with the Bengal Nagpur Railway

---

[80] Based on Sanyal, *ibid.*

(BNR), was a direct fallout of the Famine Commission Report of 1880, though work on it had started in 1878. There was a temporary problem though. There was a cap on how much the government of India could spend on productive public works, if that expenditure was based on borrowed capital. There were colonial interests towards the north-west, the Afghan Wars being a case in point. Hence, within the constraint set by that cap, the north-west was a priority, and other parts of the country got relatively less attention. Though the first line of the Nagpur Chhattisgarh Railway opened in 1880, discussions about bringing in landlocked regions like Chhattisgarh into the railway network had started to surface in the 1860s itself. An Irish geologist named Valentine Ball joined the Geological Survey of India in 1864. Since he knew so much about the central parts of India, the government asked him about a possible railway route between Bombay and Calcutta that would cut through Chhattisgarh. In 1880, Valentine Ball authored a book,[81] in which he wrote:

> While travelling along this road I paid a good deal of attention to the question of the suitability of the country between Chaibassa and Sambalpur, as a route for a direct line of railway between Calcutta and Nagpur, so avoiding the present circuitous route via Allahabad. It would be of little interest to my readers perhaps to give

---

[81] *Jungle Life in India; or the Journeys and Journals of an Indian Geologist*, Valentine Ball, Thos. De La Rue and Company, London, 1880, http://www.archive.org/stream/junglelifeinindi00balluoft#page/n7/mode/2up

the details of these observations, but I may say that I embodied them in a report, in which I pointed out that there were no serious engineering difficulties to be encountered, and that the following advantages would accrue from the construction of such a line. In the first place the possession of an alternative route could not fail to be of great strategical importance. Secondly, from six to ten hours, according to the actual route taken, would be saved on the journey from Calcutta to Bombay. Thirdly, the cheap grain of the Central Provinces could be brought to the port of Calcutta.

Table 2: Lines opened in 1881–82

Lines Open to Traffic	Supervising entity
Imperial state lines of Scindia, Punjab Northern, Indus valley, Kandhar Railways	Director-General of Railways
East Indian, Eastern Bengal, Oudh Rohilkhand, and Sindh Punjab and Delhi Railways	Government of India (Railway branch of the PWD)
Madras and South Indian Railways	Government of Madras
GIP (including Dhond–Manmad and Berar state lines), BB and CI, Rajputana, Western Rajputana, Holkar and Scindia–Neemuch, Bhabnagar–Gondal and Gaekwar Railways	Government of Bombay

Lines Open to Traffic	Supervising entity
Calcutta and South Eastern, Nalhati, Northern Bengal, Tirhut, Patna–Gaya lines	Government of Bengal
Muttra–Hathras, Kanpur–Farukkabad, Dildarnagar Railways	Government of North Western Provinces and Oudh
Wardah, Coal and Nagpur–Chattisgarh lines	Central Provinces Government
Khamgaon, Amraoti and Nizam State lines	Resident at Hyderabad
Mysore State Railways	Resident at Mysore

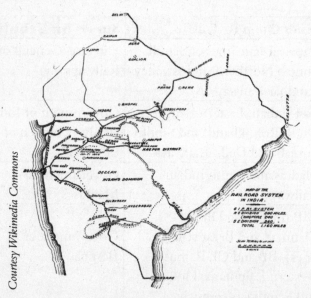

Railway network at the time of the Famine Commission
Report (1880)

Since Valentine Ball travelled quite a bit by train, his book also has other stray remarks on travel by train in those days.

'On this, my first trip up country, I was much struck by the number of third-class passengers in the train. Only on the occasion of special excursions would a similar number be seen in England. It appeared to me a most marvellous fact that a people, so averse from innovation of any kind, should have taken so universally to train travelling; and to judge from their faces they seemed thoroughly to enjoy it.' Though another quote in the book sounds apparently contradictory, there is no real contradiction, since the references are to two distinct segments of Indians. 'The road between these places lies parallel and close to the railway. With each passing train the elephant became very excited and difficult to manage, much to the delight of the engine-drivers, who maliciously turned on their whistles. A constant stream of foot-passengers from Upper India passed along this road. Whether they were forced by poverty, or had other reasons for not using the train, I cannot say. A native, to whom time is not of much value, could live at a less cost for a month, while he walked say 600 miles, than his fare for that distance, even at the low rates charged for third class, would amount to; and hence it is that many whose funds are low, start off on foot for Calcutta, where they hope to obtain service.'

In 1882, an estimated 1.39 per cent of passengers travelled first class, 1.74 per cent second class and 98 per cent third class. Freight traffic primarily shipped commodities like cotton, hides, tea, salt, oilseeds, wheat, jaggery, sugar, piece-goods and tobacco.[82] But then, as is also the case now, the passenger part was more important than the freight business.

The Secretary of State appointed a Parliamentary Select Committee in 1884. The resultant report led to the adoption of a combination of measures. First, there was a modified guarantee system, less tilted in favour of private companies. One could say that the guaranteed return was reduced to between 3 per cent and 3.5 per cent, but that would be a simplification. There were individual variations, and in some cases the guaranteed return was higher, at 4 per cent. For companies that were formed under this new system, the lines would be owned by the state, but would be constructed and operated by the companies. The contracts would be reviewed at the end of twenty-five years, or at intervals of ten years. It wasn't as if there was a great deal of demand from companies for this new system. Only three such companies—the Southern Mahratta Railway (1882), the Indian Midland Railway (1885) and the Bengal Nagpur Railway (1887) responded. However, the original proposal for the Southern Mahratta Railway went back to 1858. The Southern Mahratta built the Bellary-Hospet line, the Londa-Goa line and the first coast-to-coast line from Marmagao to Beswada. In 1886, it took over the management of the Mysore State Railway and in 1908, the Southern Mahratta Railway was merged with the Madras Railway to form the Madras and Southern Mahratta Railway. The Indian Midland Railway didn't last long. Formed in 1885, it built

---

[82] Sanyal, *op. cit.*

lines from Jhansi, and in 1900, was merged with the GIPR. Formed in 1887, the BNR had a much more distinguished history. In 1888, it bought the Nagpur Chhattisgarh Railway from the GIPR and converted it into broad gauge, the idea being a shorter Howrah–Bombay route than the one via Allahabad. The BNR also constructed the Howrah–Chennai trunk route. The BNR eventually became part of the South Eastern Railway.

A centenary postage stamp of the South Eastern Railway, commemorating the establishment of the BNR in 1887

Courtesy IRFCA

Second, some companies were formed without any guarantees. The Bengal Central Railway, formed in 1881 with the intention of constructing the Bangaon–Khulna line, via Jessore, is an example. It did construct some lines, but sub-contracted the operations to the Eastern Bengal Railway Company (EBRC). This company had been formed in 1857 to build a Calcutta–Dacca link, with a side line to Jessore. In 1884, the Eastern Bengal Railway Company was taken over by the government of India when contracts under the old guarantee system were reviewed, and became the East Bengal State Railway (EBSR). Eventually, the Bengal Central Railway was also merged with the EBSR. By 1904, several railway companies were merged into the EBSR. The Brahmaputra–Sultanpur Railway (opened in 1899), the Calcutta and South Eastern Railway (opened in 1862), the Cooch Behar State Railway (opened in 1893), the Dacca State Railway (opened in 1885), the Kaunia–Dharnia State Tram/Railway (opened in 1884–85), the Kaunia–Kurigram Railway (opened in 1885), Mymensingh–Jamalpur–Jagannath Railway (opened in 1898 and owned by the Indian General Navigation and Railway Company), the Northern Bengal State Railway (opened in 1877), the Ranaghat–Krishnanagar Light Railway (opened in 1899) and the Santipur–Nabadwip Light Railway (opened in 1898) were some of them.

There were other companies that were taken over by the East Bengal State Railway later, after 1904. As the list above illustrates, these companies were simply not viable. The Bengal and North Western Railway, registered in 1882, didn't have guarantees either. Nor did the Rohilkhand and Kumaun Railway, also registered in 1882.

Third, as has just been mentioned, in some cases, when it was time to renew contracts under the old guarantee system, those railways were acquired by the government. This is what happened with the East Bengal Railway Company. Initially, the demarcation between the footprints of the East Bengal Railway Company and the East Indian Railway Company (EIRC) was the River Hooghly. The EBRC was supposed to operate on the eastern side of the river, and the EIRC on the western side. Before it was taken over in 1884, the EBRC built the Calcutta–Kushtia line in 1862. Once it was taken over, the EBRC became the East Bengal State Railway. (The name changed to the East Bengal Railway in 1915.) One of the remarkable feats, which linked what was happening on the east of the Hooghly with what was happening on its west, was the linking of the East Bengal Railway Company's lines with those of the East Indian Railway Company. This happened when the Jubilee Bridge linking Bandel and Nalhati was opened in 1887, the construction having taken five years. This cantilever bridge was called the Jubilee Bridge because it was opened to coincide with Queen Victoria's silver jubilee coronation celebrations.

The Oudh and Rohilkhand Railway had been established in 1872, using the assets of the Indian Branch Railway Company. It operated under the old guarantee system. The division between the Oudh and Rohilkhand Railway and the East Indian Railway Company (EIRC) was reasonably clear. The EIRC would operate south of the Ganges and the Oudh and Rohilkhand Railway would usually, though not invariably, operate north of the Ganges. In 1888, the government of India took over the Oudh and Rohilkhand Railway. Before that, in 1887, the Oudh and Rohilkhand Railway had opened a double-decker bridge over the Ganges in Varanasi. Known as Dufferin Bridge, it was subsequently renamed the Malaviya Bridge in 1948 after Pandit Madan Mohan Malaviya. As with the Jubilee Bridge, the Dufferin Bridge connected the lines of the Oudh and Rohilkhand Railway with those of the East Indian Railway Company at Mughal Sarai. The Dufferin in question is Lord Dufferin, who became Viceroy in 1884. Interestingly, Rudyard

Kipling wrote a poem titled 'One Viceroy Resigns'. This was in the form of advice given by Lord Dufferin to his successor, Lord Lansdowne. This is interesting because the railways featured in Kipling's writings, including his fiction. One such story, published in 1893, is titled 'The Bridge-Builders'. This is about a bridge being built across the Ganges. The story begins,

> The least that Findlayson, of the Public Works Department, expected was a C.I.E.; he dreamed of a C.S.I. Indeed, his friends told him that he deserved more. For three years he had endured heat and cold, disappointment, discomfort, danger, and disease, with responsibility almost too top-heavy for one pair of shoulders; and day by day, through that time, the great Kashi Bridge over the Ganges had grown under his charge. Now, in less than three months, if all went well, his Excellency the Viceroy would open the bridge in state, an archbishop would bless it, and the first trainload of soldiers would come over it, and there would be speeches.[83]

Since there is a reference to Kashi and also to a flood, which the Dufferin Bridge too had to encounter during its construction, this story is believed to be based on the Dufferin Bridge, although the actual description of the bridge doesn't bear any resemblance to it.

---

[83] http://www.telelib.com/authors/K/KiplingRudyard/prose/TheDaysWork/bridgebuilders.html

To return to the acquisitions, the Scinde, Punjab and Delhi Railway Company was also acquired by the government of India in 1885.

Today there are 1,38,912 bridges in the Indian Railways system. Some of them are old bridges that go back to the second half of the nineteenth century; 54,000 are more than 100 years old; and 75,000 more than eighty years old. The original builders and engineers typically gave these bridges fitness certificates for 100 years. In 1999, there was a Railway Safety Review Committee under the chairmanship of Justice H.R. Khanna. This identified 527 bridges as weak and distressed, 262 being identified as distressed. That is, they were in urgent need of repair. What's remarkable is that the bridges should have lasted this long. Their suffering distress, with the passage of time, is understandable.

The opening of the Jubilee Bridge in 1887

The Dufferin Bridge

Courtesy IRFCA by Vikas Singh

Fourth, some railway companies were acquired by the government, but their management remained with the private railway companies, through a lease. This is what happened with the East Indian Railway Company (acquired in 1879) and the Great Indian Peninsula Railway (acquired in 1900).

Courtesy National Rail Museum, Delhi

Churchgate station, 1876

These different structures illustrate the complexity of the railway companies in the country.

Fifth, to complicate matters further, there were the native or princely state railways. There were several princely states or native states in India, and they had a subsidiary kind of alliance with the government of India. They were not directly governed by the British. At the time of Independence in 1947, there were 565 princely states. As is natural, there was a great deal of variation among these states. We tend to think of the larger railway companies and don't realize that there were many such companies. Initially, the British didn't consider the prospect of railways constructed by native or princely states seriously. After all, railway construction was largely designed to achieve a political end, and the princely states didn't fit into this mould. Attitudes changed when the fiscal costs of the old guarantee system started to manifest. The British then started to encourage the princely states to build their own railways, and there were several such started in the 1870s. We have provided a list of some of these railways.[84] Our intention is not to give a complete and exhaustive list; instead, we want to drive home the point that there were many more princely state railways than is commonly assumed. After all, at the time of Independence in 1947, there were in excess of 550 princely states, and several of them had their own railways.

---

[84] http://wiki.fibis.org/index.php/Category:Indian_States_
Railways

1. The Agra–Gwalior Railway: This was subsequently renamed the Gwalior Light Railway. Owned by Gwalior State, this narrow gauge network was operated by the GIPR. In 1944, it was renamed the Scindia State Railway.

Courtesy IRFCA by Vikas Singh

The Gwalior Light Railway

2. The Ati–Kunch Branch Railway: This was opened in 1897. It was first operated by the Indian Midland Railway and then by the GIPR.

3. The Amraoti State Railway: A metre-gauge line between Amraoti and Baderna, opened in 1871 and operated by GIPR.

4. The Anandapuram–Sagara Railway: This is of later vintage (1938), an extension of the Birur–Shimoga Railway and operated by the Mysore State Railway.

5. The Anklesvar–Rajpipla Railway: This was a narrow gauge line opened in 1897, owned by Rajpipla State. This line was constructed and operated by the Bombay, Baroda and Central India Railway (BBCIR). In 1899, it was renamed the Rajpipla State Railway.

6. The Assam–Behar State Railway: This was jointly owned by the Assam and Behar States. The Parantipur–Katihar line was constructed between 1884 and 1889 and was probably (though this is not known for sure) operated by the Assam Bengal Railway.

7. The Bahawalnagar–Fort Abbas Railway: This line between Bahawalnagar and Fort Abbas was built considerably later, in 1928. It was owned by the Bahawalpur State and operated by the North Western Railway.

8. The Bahawalpur Royal Railway: Built in 1911, this was also known as the Khanpur–Chachran Railway. It was owned by the Bahawalpur State and operated by the North Western Railway.

9. The Balharshah–Warangal Railway: Opened between 1924 and 1928, it was part of what came to be known as the Nizam's State Railway. The British may have persuaded the Nizam of Hyderabad to part with capital for construction of the railways, but they soon lost control of what was going on. The Nizam contributed 1 million pounds for a Wadi–Hyderabad line that was opened in 1874. Initially, this was operated by the GIPR. However, these soon started to operate as the Nizam's Railway, and in 1883, the Nizam established the Nizam's Guaranteed Railway as a management company. In other words, the Nizam soon had his network and his own system of guarantees for companies. At various points in time, several railway lines have been part of the Nizam's Guaranteed Railway system. These include the Balharshah–Warangal Railway, the Bezwada Extension

Railway, the Hingoli Branch Railway, the Hyderabad–Godavari Valley Railway, the Karepalli–Kothagudem Railway, the Kazipet–Balharshah Railway, the Parbhani–Purli Railway, the Purna Junction–Hingoli Railway, the Secunderabad–Gadwal Railway and the Singareni Coal Fields Railway.

The Nizam's Guaranteed State Railway logo

Courtesy S.C.R. Ruby Jubilee Exhibition, IRFCA

10. The Bangalore Harihar Railway: Opened in 1889, this was part of the Mysore State Railway system.

11. The Bangalore Hindupur Railway: Oddly enough, although this railway did exist, nothing very much is known about it.

12. The Baria State Railway: This narrow gauge line was owned by Baria State and was opened in 1892. Subsequently, it became the Baria–Piplod State Railway. The BBCIR operated the line.

13. The Baroda State Railway: Gaekwar has the distinction of being the first princely state to develop a railway. This is partly because the Maharaja of Gaekwar realized the commercial importance of the town of Dabhoi (Darbhavati) and the enhanced benefits a better transportation network would bring

to Dabhoi and to the region. Initially, in 1862, there was something called the Gaekwar's Dabhoi Railway. A narrow gauge line was laid between Dabhoi and Miyagam Karjan (twenty miles away), and a pair of oxen hauled the trains. When steam locomotives were introduced in 1863, the lines couldn't handle them. Therefore, the lines had to be laid again, and when the railway was reopened in 1873, it came to be known as the Gaekwar's Baroda Railway. Soon, there were several narrow and metre gauge lines throughout Baroda State, and these were merged to form the Gaekwar's Baroda State Railway.

Courtesy Wikimedia Commons

Initial days of the Baroda State Railway

14. The Bhavnagar State Railway: This was a metre gauge line, opened in 1880, owned by Bhavnagar State.

15. The Bhavnagar–Gondal–Junagad–Porbandar Railway: This was a cluster of metre gauge lines, opened in the 1890s and owned by the states of Bhavnagar, Gondal, Junagad and Porbandar.

16. The Bhopal State Railway: This belonged to Bhopal State and was a link between Bhopal and the GIPR

line, at Itarsi. It was opened in 1884, and was operated by the Indian Midland Railway. Thereafter, it became the Bhopal–Itarsi Railway. In 1900, it became part of the GIPR.

17. The Bhopal–Ujjain Railway: A broad gauge line owned by Bhopal State and opened in 1895, it linked Bhopal with Ujjain. It was operated by the Indian Midland Railway and then became part of the GIPR in 1900.

18. The Bikaner State Railway: This was a metre gauge line, opened in 1924 and jointly operated and owned by Bikaner State and Jodhpur State.

19. The Bina–Goona–Baran Railway: A broad gauge line owned by Gwalior State, opened in 1899 and operated by the GIPR.

20. The Birur–Shimoga Railway: This was a metre gauge line opened in 1899, owned by Mysore State and worked by the Southern Mahratta Railway.

21. The Bodeli–Chhota Udaipur Railway: This was a later line, opened in 1917–18. It was a narrow gauge line and an extension of the Gaekwar's Dabhoi Railway. Constructed and operated by the BBCIR, it was owned by Baroda State.

22. The Chickjajur–Chitaldurg Railway: This metre gauge line, also opened later, in 1921, was owned by Mysore State. It was operated by the Mysore State Railway.

23. The Cooch Behar State Railway: This was a narrow gauge line, constructed in 1894 and owned by Cooch Behar State. It was operated by the Eastern Bengal Railway.

24. The Cutch State Railway: This was a narrow gauge line, with the first sections started in 1903. It was constructed, financed and operated by Kutch State.

25. The Dholpur–Bari State Railway: This was opened in 1908, a narrow gauge line owned and operated by Dholpur State. It connected Dholpur to the Jhansi–Agra GIPR line. Subsequently, this was renamed the Dholpur State Railway.

26. The Dhrangadhra Railway: This was a metre gauge line, owned by Dhrangadhra State. Started in 1898, it was first operated by the Bhavnagar–Gondal–Junagad–Porbandar Railway and later by the Bhavnagar State Railways.

27. The Gondal State Railway: This was a metre gauge line, owned by the Gondal State, opened in 1881 and operated by Bhavnagar–Gondal–Junagad–Porbandar Railway, at least initially. Subsequently, in 1911, it was jointly operated by the Porbandar State Railway, thus constituting the Gondal–Porbandar Railway.

28. The Hindupur–Yesvantpur Railway: This metre gauge line was part of a Guntakal–Bangalore link, and was opened in 1893. It was owned by Mysore State and was initially operated by the Southern Mahratta Railway. Here one is led to the big-picture story of the Mysore State Railway (MSR). The Chennai–Bengaluru railway line slices through the town of Jolarpettai/Jollarpet. The Madras Railway constructed the Royapuram (Madras)–Wallajah Road (Arcot) railway line in 1856. Subsequently, in

1864, the Wallajah Road–Bangalore Cantonment line started to be built, and it went via Jollarpettai, which thus expanded along both sides of the line. One must also mention the station known as Bowringpet, now renamed as Bangarapet. The station was named after Lewin Bowring, who is almost forgotten today. For a while, Bowring was the Chief Commissioner of Mysore State. If one intends to go to the Kolar Gold Fields, one needs to change at Bowringpet/Bangarapet, which is on the Chennai–Bengaluru line. Lewin Bowring also sought to push the idea of establishing railroad connectivity between the Madras Presidency and Mysore State. The first sections of the MSR were built during 1876–77, as a famine relief measure. This was the Bangalore–Mysore railway line, constructed by the Maharaja (Wadiyar) of Mysore. This line was opened in 1881–82. However, the Mysore State had incurred a considerable amount of debt, and it leased out the line to the Southern Mahratta Railway for a period of forty-five years. When the Southern Mahratta Railway became the Madras and Southern Mahratta Railway in 1907, the Mysore State again started to construct railway lines itself. The leased Bangalore–Mysore line was returned to it in 1919. At different points in time, different railways have been part of the MSR system. Other than Mysore State Railway itself, there were the Anandapuram–Sagara Railway, the Birur–Shimoga Railway, the Bowringpet–Chikballapur

Railway, the Chickjajur–Chitaldurg Railway, the Chikballapur–Bangalore City Railway, the Mysore–Arsikere Railway, Mysore–Nanjangud Railway, the Nanjangud–Chamrajnagar Railway, the Shimoga–Anandapuram Railway, the Tadassa–Hebbe Tramway and the Tarikere–Narasimharajapura Tramway.

29. Holkar and Scindia–Neemuch Railway: In 1874, a Holkar State Railway was started as a metre gauge line from Khandwa to Indore. The main GIPR line passed through Khandwa. The Holkar State Railway was owned by Holkar State and was initially operated as the Holkar and Scindia-Neemuch Railway. As with the Nizam of Hyderabad, the British managed to persuade the Maharajas of Holkar and Scindia to put in money. The Maharaja of Holkar offered 1 million sterling for the Khandwa–Indore line. The British government promised him an interest rate of 4.5 per cent and half a share in all surplus profits. The Khandwa–Indore alignment was a difficult one as it had to cross the Narmada and negotiate steep gradients along the Vindhya Ghats, with slopes as steep as 1:40. The bridge across the Narmada was built with the use of piers. It was named the Holkar Narmada Bridge and was opened in 1876. Meanwhile, for the Indore–Ujjain–Neemuch segment, the Maharaja of Scindia offered Rs 75 lakh, at an interest rate of 4 per cent. In 1872–73, the Scindia-Neemuch Railway started to operate on these finances. From 1874, the Holkar Railway and the Scindia-Neemuch Railway started to operate jointly as the Holkar and Scindia-Neemuch Railway.

Courtesy National Rail Museum, Delhi

Maharaja Gaekwar's salon

30. The Rajputana–Malwa State Railway: It wasn't just
     the British who turned to the railways to deal with
     the spectre of famines. Princely states too looked
     to the railways as a relief measure against famine
     and drought. The railways would serve to establish
     transport connectivity to remote places. The
     Rajputana–Malwa State Railway wasn't a railway
     constructed by princely states, at least not in its
     entirety. It was initially called the Rajputana State
     Railway, the first metre gauge railway and also the
     first railway to be constructed by the government
     of India, between the years 1873 and 1875. Initially,
     Delhi was linked to Agra via Alwar and Bandikui.
     Subsequently, the line was extended up to Ajmer, the
     intention being to extend it up to Ahmedabad so as to
     link it to the broad gauge BBCIR network. However,

the province of Ajmer–Merwara, understandably, desired that there should be a Marwar–Pali–Jodhpur railway line, and contributed Rs 3 lakh as security for a survey and expenses. The Rajputana–Malwa State Railway built this line in 1885. But some of the lines were constructed for the Rajputana–Malwa Railway by the Jodhpur–Bikaner Railway. This was a metre gauge system, jointly owned and operated by Jodhpur State and Bikaner State. We have now digressed a bit. The Rajputana State Railway became the Rajputana–Malwa State Railway in 1881–82, amalgamating the Rajputana State Railway, the Holkar State Railway, the Scindia-Neemuch Railway, the Neemuch Nasirabad State Railway and the Western Rajputana State Railway. However, the lines were operated by BBCIR. Eventually, in 1900, the Rajputana Malwa State Railway was also absorbed by the BBCIR.

Clearly, the railway network had a positive impact on dampening the scourge of famines and drought in Rajasthan. In 1894, George Herbert Trevor authored a book, *Rhymes of Rajputana*,[85] which was, as the title implies, a collection of poems on various aspects of Rajputana/Rajasthan—its lifestyle, culture, traditions and history. One of these poems was titled 'Famine in Rajputana, 1892'; it spoke about how the iron horse had saved Rajasthan from famines.

---

[85] *Rhymes of Rajputana*, George Herbert Trevor, Macmillan and Company, London, 1894.

The Goddess of Chittor in olden time
Craved regal victims – superstition tells:
But this gaunt spectre ravages and dwells
Among the poor, in poverty and slime,
Tempting despair and maddening to crime.
We read in former days how dried-up well
And barren fields brought death;
Old chronicles
Speak of slain hecatombs: but now like chime of
bells
O'er hills the railways' scream is heard.
The Iron Horse has saved the land and scared
The spectre Famine, like some bird
Disturbed at its foul feast.
Had God but spared
The poor man's cattle, ah, what joy had stirred
The hearts of those for whom in need He cared.

31. The Jammu and Kashmir Railway: A broad gauge
    line from Sialkot to Jammu, opened in 1890, and
    owned by Kashmir State.

32. The Mourbhanj Railway: This was a narrow gauge
    line, opened in 1905, linking Rupea to Baripada. It was
    owned by Mourbhanj State and operated by BNR.
    Subsequently, in 1920, this was renamed the Mayurbhanj
    Railway. A Baripada–Talbond Railway, with a narrow
    gauge line from Baripada to Talbond, was added in 1920.

33. The Parlakimedi Light Railway: This was a narrow
    gauge line, opened in 1900, connecting Parlakimedi
    to Nanpada. It was owned by Parlakimedi State.

34. The Patiala State Monorail Trainways: This was functional from 1907 to 1927, and was remarkable because it was a monorail system. This monorail was based on what is called the Ewing System, after the name of its inventor, W.J. Ewing. Interestingly, the only two places in the world where this Ewing System monorail seems to have been used are both in India. Patiala State Monorail Trainways had two separate lines, one from Sirhind to Morinda and the second from Patiala to Sunam. Patiala State owned 560 mules. Initially, these mules, and also bullocks, were used to haul the monorail. Eventually, however, steam traction took over. The second monorail was the Kundala Valley Railway. This was owned by a plantation company in Kundala Valley, near Munnar in Kerala. It was functional from 1902 to 1908, and closed down thereafter. However, Kundala Valley Railway only used bullocks. Unlike Patiala State Monorail Trainways, it never switched to steam traction.

Patiala State Monorail Trainways, National Railway Museum, New Delhi

The railways began to expand in a different geographical sense too, courtesy the mountain railways, though only one of these actually goes back to the nineteenth century. The mountain railways reflected the Hyde Clarke idea of ruling from the hills. The Darjeeling Himalayan Railway (DHR) was the one constructed in the nineteenth century. By 1878, there was a broad gauge line from Calcutta to Siliguri, in the foothills of the Himalayas. The Eastern Bengal Railway Company proposed a steam tramway from Siliguri to Darjeeling, along Hill Cart Road; this was a road from Siliguri to Darjeeling that was known first as Cart Road, since horse carts travelled along it, and later, as Hill Cart Road. Once the idea was accepted by the government, construction started. The Siliguri–Kurseong stretch was opened in 1880, and the section up to Darjeeling in 1881. Because of the steep gradient, the DHR had several loops and Z-reverses where the train moves along the shape of a 'Z' and reverses. Some of the loops along the DHR, such as the Batasia Loop, not far from Darjeeling, are famous. However, the tightest curve along the DHR is another loop, known as Agony Point. Somewhat later, in 1923, Lord Ronaldshay had the following to say:[86]

> Siliguri is palpably a place of meeting... The discovery that here the metre gauge system ends and the two-foot gauge of the Darjeeling-Himalayan railway begins, confirms what all these things hint at . . .

[86] *Lands of the Thunderbolt: Sikkim, Chumbi, and Bhutan*, Ronaldshay, SLG Books, 1923.

One steps into a railway carriage which might easily be mistaken for a toy, and the whimsical idea seizes hold of one that one has accidentally stumbled into Lilliput. With a noisy fuss out of all proportion to its size the engine gives a jerk—and starts . . . No special mechanical device such as a rack is employed—unless, indeed, one can so describe the squat and stolid hill-man who sits perched over the forward buffers of the engine and scatters sand on the rails when the wheels of the engine lose their grip of the metals and race, with the noise of a giant spring running down when the control has been removed. Sometimes we cross our own track after completing the circuit of a cone, at others we zigzag backwards and forwards; but always we climb at a steady gradient—so steady that if one embarks in a trolley at Ghum, the highest point on the line, the initial push supplies all the energy necessary to carry one to the bottom.

Courtesy IRFCA

Agony Point along the Darjeeling Himalayan Railway

The Nilgiri Mountain Railway was proposed as early as in 1854, but it didn't get constructed until much later. Unlike most other mountain railways, this was a metre gauge line. Work started in 1894 and was completed in stages, between 1899 and 1908, though it was formally inaugurated by Lord Curzon only in 1903. The Nilgiri Mountain Railway is the only railway in India to have ever used the alternate biting system (Abt), commonly known as the rack and pinion system. (It is used for part of the line, not all of it.) Three of India's mountain railways have obtained World Heritage status from UNESCO. The Darjeeling Himalayan Railway (DHR) got this status in 1999, the Nilgiri Mountain Railway (NMR) in 2005 and the Kalka–Shimla Railway (KSR) in 2008. An application from the Matheran Hill Railway (MHR) for World Heritage status has been pending with UNESCO (the 2009 attempt failed). The submission for World Heritage status by the Nilgiri Mountain Railway flags this unique rack and pinion system and carries an excellent description of what this entails.[87]

The NMR is a rack and adhesion Railway. Rack and adhesion Railways are mixed technology. They combine conventional sections of Railway, where traction is provided through the wheels of the locomotives on the rail (adhesion) and,

---

[87] http://whc.unesco.org/uploads/nominations/944bis.pdf

where grades are too steep for this, sections where traction is provided by cog wheels (pinions) on the locomotive, which engage a rack, laid in the centre of the tracks. It is this mixture of technology, and their consequent ability to carry considerable traffic in conventional rolling stock, which differentiates them from rack Railways pure and simple, where no traction is provided by adhesion. Rack Railways were built to enable Railways to penetrate extremely inhospitable and steep terrain, which would not be accessible to conventional adhesion Railways ... Most rack and adhesion Railways were built in the last decade of the nineteenth and the first of the twentieth century, and the NMR is no exception. By the time rack and adhesion technology was mature, the motor age was dawning, and roads rather than Railways have been the normal means of access to such locations.

We have Guilford Molesworth to thank for this unique rack and pinion system. He was a consulting engineer (on railways) to the government of India, and submitted a report in 1886 advocating this rack and pinion or Abt system.

The Kalka–Shimla Railway, the third of the World Heritage Indian mountain railways, was finally opened in 1903, but the surveys for possible alternative routes had commenced in the mid-1880s. The

Delhi–Ambala–Kalka Railway Company built this narrow gauge line. There are several tunnels and bridges along the line, the most famous of the tunnels being the Barog tunnel, conventionally tunnel number 33. This is named after a railway engineer, Colonel Barog, and thereby hangs a tale. The tunnelling that had started from both ends was supposed to meet in the middle. Unfortunately, the alignments went wrong, and the borings did not meet in the middle. Consequently, a fine of Re 1 was imposed on Barog. Shamed at the ignominy, Barog shot himself and his dog. His grave is up a hill, right next to the Barog tunnel. Barog's ghost is still believed to haunt the tunnel. After this episode, the tunnel was still incomplete, and the task was assigned to H.S. Harrington, the chief engineer.

History gets mixed with legend when it comes to what happened next. Here a character called Bhalku, also known as Baba Bhalku, or Sadhu Bhalku as in the plaque shown in the image below, joined the team. He possessed the uncanny ability of tapping on the mountain wall with a wooden staff, and, depending on the sound that it yielded, instructing the team where to dig. This was how the Barog Tunnel was eventually completed. Baba Bhalku used the same principle for all the other tunnels that needed to be built on the Kalka–Shimla Railway. There must have been some truth in all this, since the British government honoured Baba Bhalku with a medal and a turban. The Railway Museum in Shimla is named after Baba Bhalku.

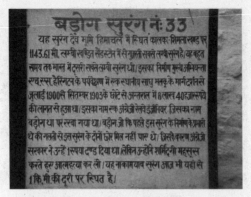

Plaque at Colonel Barog's grave

The Baba Bhalku story is slightly reminiscent of another story from the BNR.[88] On the Grand Chord line, there lies the station of Talgoria. As the track approaches the platform, it veers sharply to the right, loops around and becomes straight again; there is also an octagonal hole in the centre of the railway platform today. There is a tale behind both the curve of the track and that hole. The track was originally meant to be straight, and indeed was straight before it approached the station of Talgoria. However, when the track began to be laid in Talgoria in the 1930s, the coolies kept falling ill and refused to work. A holy man came and explained what was going on. There was a '*suttee*' site there, and it would be impossible to lay a track without bypassing that sacred spot, pronounced the holy man. As a result, the track makes a detour and, as for the octagonal hole, it represents the sacred site.

---

[88] Quoted in, *South Eastern Railway, March to New Millennium*, R.R. Bhandari, South Eastern Railway, 2001.

The Barog tunnel

Though the Darjeeling–Himalayan, Nilgiri Mountain
and Kalka–Shimla lines are the best known mountain
railways in the country, they weren't the only ones.
Between 1904 and 1907, the Adamjee group constructed
the Matheran Hill Railway, between Neral and Matheran
in the Western Ghats. There is only one tunnel along this
route, going by the rather unusual name of 'One Kiss
Tunnel'. That's because this is a short tunnel, and as the
train passes through, there is just enough time to give your
partner one kiss and no more. The Kangra Valley Railway
is also a mountain railway, but was built much later, in
the 1920s. Though not as famous as the other mountain
railways, it expanded into the hill section, making for the
Lumding-Halflong-Badarpur stretch, a metre gauge line,
built in the 1890s by what was then the Assam Bengal
Railway. Other than people, tea, coal and timber from
upper Assam were shipped on this line, from where the
goods were eventually the go to Chittagong port. Though
building started in the 1890s, it was opened for operations

only in 1904. There were thirty-seven tunnels on this stretch. Near Jatinga, there was also the steepest railway gradient in the world. Construction wasn't easy.[89]

There are other interesting trivia too, about the railways in India. In September 1894, an elephant tried to cross the railway track at Goikera—in the West Singhum district of what is today Jharkhand, where the Saranda forest lies—and the UP Mail ran into him. The elephant died. One of its tusks is in London, in what used to be the office of the East India Railway Company. Another tusk was claimed by James Bell, the engine driver. The rest of the skull is in the National Railway Museum.

Courtesy National Rail Museum, Delhi

The Neral–Matheran Railway in its early days

---

[89] See the description in *Indian Railways, the Final Frontier: Genesis and Growth of the North-East Frontier Railway*, Arup Kumar Dutta, North East Frontier Railway, 2002.

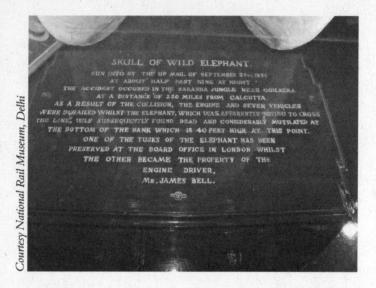

Courtesy National Rail Museum, Delhi

The elephant skull at the National Rail Museum

As the railway network spread, services on trains improved. There is an oft-quoted—and therefore somewhat clichéd—letter, written by Okhil Chandra Sen to the Divisional Superintendent of Sahibganj in 1909, familiar to all those who are familiar with Indian railway history. The original letter is in the National Railway Museum, Delhi. This led to the introduction of toilets on trains, or so runs the assertion. This self-explanatory letter read:

> Dear Sir, I am arrive by passenger train Ahmedpur station and my belly is too much swelling with jackfruit. I am therefore went to privy. Just I doing the nuisance that guard making whistle blow for train to go off and I am running with LOTAH in one hand &

DHOTI in the next when I am fall over & expose all
my shocking to men & female women on platform.
I am got leaved Ahmedpur station. This too much
bad, if passenger go to make dung that dam guard not
wait train minutes for him. I am therefor pray your
honour to make big fine on that guard for public sake.
Otherwise I am making big report to papers.

Sahibganj (in Jharkhand) has seen better days, from the
railways' point of view. It is no longer on the Howrah–Delhi
main line. Ahmedpur is in West Bengal, and Sen must have
travelled along the Bardhman–Sainthia section of what is
called the Sahibganj loop. The assertion about this letter
leading to toilets on trains is not true. The upper class section
began to have toilets on trains in the 1870s. The Sen letter
probably led to the introduction of toilets in the lower class
sections. However, for a long time, toilets in the lower class
compartments had no lights and no running water. For the
sake of accuracy, the veracity of the Sen letter is questionable.

There was a distinct segregation between the classes.
Kipling wrote a lot about the railways, and that such
segregation existed is extremely clear in his work.[90]

The beginning of everything was in a railway train
upon the road to Mhow from Ajmir. There had been
a deficit in the Budget, which necessitated travelling,
not Second-class, which is only half as dear as First-

---

[90] *The Man Who Would Be King*, Rudyard Kipling, 1888, Indian
Railway Library, is a very good example.

class, but by Intermediate, which is very awful indeed. There are no cushions in the Intermediate class, and the population are either Intermediate, which is Eurasian, or native, which for a long night journey is nasty; or Loafer, which is amusing though intoxicated. Intermediates do not patronize refreshment-rooms. They carry their food in bundles and pots, and buy sweets from the native sweetmeat-sellers, and drink the roadside water. That is why in the hot weather Intermediates are taken out of the carriages dead, and in all weathers are most properly looked down upon.

Though the complaints would become even more acute in the twentieth century, even in the nineteenth century there were complaints about the differential treatment meted out to Indian passengers.

There was a lot about the railways that was not standardized, at least not until the first Indian Railway Conference in 1871. Today we sometimes don't remember the variations that existed, and too often, a discussion of the history of the railways in India ignores these aspects.[91] For instance, the railway companies not only had their own timetables, they often followed their own local standard times.[92] Broadly, all companies towards the west followed 'Bombay Time' and all those towards the

---

[91] *Wheels of Change? Impact of railways on colonial north Indian society, 1855-1920*, Aparajita Mukhopadhyay, PhD dissertation, Department of History, School of Oriental and African Studies, University of London, is an exception. This section draws on that dissertation.

[92] The EIRC was the first railway company to have a published timetable, with fares included. This was in 1854.

east followed 'Calcutta Time'. For a while, 'Madras Time', which was in between, was followed. All this was before Indian Standard Time was formally adopted in 1905. When there were timetables, trains didn't adhere to the indicated timings. When we think of the differential treatment meted out to Indian passengers, we tend to think in terms of classes of travel. In general, there was first class, second/intermediate class, third class and even fourth class. That 1871 Railway Conference sought to bring about some standardization in the carriage system. The Pullman Car Company, established by George Pullman in 1862, started to build better carriages, with sleeper berths for passengers. The story goes that George Pullman was driven to do this when he spent an uncomfortable night on a Buffalo-Westfield train trip. The Pullman carriages allowed upper berths to be folded up and down. Since first and second class were used by British and European passengers, the 1871 Conference decided that these should have Pullman carriages. An exception was made for Indian women though, since there were second class family compartments exclusively meant for them. However, there were also third class family compartments and third class all-women compartments.[93] Better passenger amenities on coaches were introduced in first and second class, but not in third class.

The French traveller, L. Rousselet, travelled by such a sleeper coach in the 1880s.[94]

---

[93] Laura Bear, *op. cit.*

[94] *India and its Native Princes. Travels in Central India and in the Presidencies of Bombay and Bengal*, L. Rousselet, Bickers, London, 1882. Quoted by IRFCA, http://www.irfca.org/docs/history/rousselet-travel-india.html

We took our tickets at Bhagulpore for Azimgange, the station for Moorshedabad. As the train left at two in the morning, we were placed in one of the comfortable sleeping-carriages which the East Indian Railway has recently introduced on its lines. These carriages contain only two compartments, in each of which there is but a single seat, the movable back of which takes off, and, being fastened by straps, forms a sort of couch of the same description as the beds used in ships' cabins. On the opposite side of the carriage are two closets one for the toilet, the other for convenience. By paying a slight addition to the price of the ordinary places, you may thus travel surrounded by all the comforts so essential in this country . . . Thanks to the sleeping-carriages, I had been able to travel over this immense distance with comparatively little fatigue sleeping at night on a comfortable little bed, and walking up and down in my carriage during the day; and at stations unprovided with buffets, I found a servant who, when he had taken the orders for my meal, telegraphed on to the next station, where my breakfast or dinner awaited my arrival . . . The Anglo-Indian Companies are making praiseworthy efforts to succeed in rendering long journeys by rail possible even in summer. Thus travelers proceeding from Bombay to Calcutta by the express trains are now accommodated with carriages with cuscas swathed in mattings, which are kept moist by reservoirs specially provided for the purpose. This moisture, enveloping the carriage, preserves the temperature at a degree of coolness sufficient almost to

> extinguish the risk of incurring sun-stroke or apoplexy,
> at one time so frequent on these journeys.

However, other accounts don't suggest that these attempts at cooling, the precursor of air conditioning, were terribly successful. Those cooling attempts came before lights on trains did. Initially, coaches had no lights and passengers had to bring their own candles and oil lamps. Experimental lighting in carriages was introduced around 1897, the Jodhpur Railway being the first, in 1902, to make it standard, at least for first class. First and second class coaches were later provided with lights and fans. The intermediate class was provided only with lights. The third class only had two lights at the two ends of the compartment, near the doors.

Before the advent of the railway network, postal services of all varieties were prohibitively expensive. Despite steamers, couriers and *dak* runners, a letter from Bombay to Calcutta took ten days to reach. In 1870, the EIRC set up a travelling post office and by 1907, there was a full-fledged railway mail service. This started the category of mail trains. As is the case now, mail and express trains were superior to other trains. However, one sometimes tends to miss the correlation between class of train and class of travel.

Those trains which ran at a slower speed, followed more inconvenient timings than the faster ones; and the bulk of 'native' passengers were forced to travel in slow trains because the faster ones did not have third or fourth class carriages. Most often, they travelled in the 'mixed' trains which were a combination of lower class carriages and goods wagons.

Meant to carry only 'native' passengers, these trains usually comprised only third and fourth class carriages and rarely (if ever) any intermediate or second class carriages. Their speed was also slow compared to the mail or the express trains. On an average a 'mixed' train ran at a speed of 16–18 kilometres per hour, while the mail or the express trains ran at a speed of 20–25 kilometres per hour. Further, the 'mixed' trains had long halts built in their schedule which made journeys longer. Passengers travelling by these trains had to pass several days in the trains before they reached their destinations.[95]

There were separate ticket booking counters for lower class travel, and tickets were only available at the major stations, not necessarily at the originating station. There were several complaints about ticket booking arrangements, including fraud by ticket booking clerks and harassment by railway police.

In Black And White. A. H. Wheeler & Co.'s Indian Railway Library No. 3 / One Rupee.

Kipling, Rudyard.

Note: This is not the actual book cover.

A 1888 Kipling publication

---

[95] Aparajita Mukhopadhyay, *op.cit.*

Many of the Kipling stories, including 'The Man Who Would Be King', were first published by the Indian Railway Library. This was a publishing concern set up by A.H. Wheeler in Allahabad in 1888; Wheeler had a monopoly on selling books at railway stations. Both the Indian Railway Library and Wheeler are part of the historical legacy of the Indian railway system. The Indian Railway Library was Kipling's idea. He needed money to fund his return to England in 1888 and for something that was a bit like a world tour. To this end he approached Emile Edouard Moreau with a proposal that his stories should be republished (they had all been published earlier) in cheap prints. Illustrated by Kipling's father, John Lockwood Kipling, six such collections were published—*Soldiers Three*, *The Story of the Gadsbys*, *In Black and White*, *Under the Deodars*, *The Phantom Rickshaw and Other Eerie Tales* and *Wee Willie Winkie and Other Child Stories*—all at Re 1 each. Nothing else was ever published by the Indian Railway Library. As for Emile Edouard Moreau—who was born in 1856—he is often unnecessarily confused with the French playwright Emile Moreau, who was born in 1877, the year when A.H. Wheeler was set up. (1877 is usually cited as the year that A.H. Wheeler & Co. was established, though 1874 is also sometimes mentioned.) Emile Edouard Moreau happened to be in Allahabad at the time because he was an employee of Bird and Company.[96] Moreau's

---

[96] See the interesting details in 'The many lives of the mysterious Emile Edouard Moreau, founder of A.H. Wheeler and Co.'

grandfather, James Bird, had also been in the bookselling business. Predictably, Moreau was fond of books, and so was his friend, Arthur Henry Wheeler. A.H. Wheeler was then in Allahabad, though he moved to London later. Back in Allahabad, A.H. Wheeler possessed a huge collection of books, too many to take back home. Since passengers, especially the upper classes, had got into the habit of reading on train journeys, Moreau volunteered to sell Wheeler's old and unwanted books from a wooden almirah in Allahabad railway station.[97] This venture was so successful that in 1877, A.H. Wheeler and Company was set up as a partnership. Arthur Henry Wheeler and Moreau weren't the only partners. There were also Arthur Lisle Wheeler, W.M. Rudge and Tigran Ratheus. The company had offices in Allahabad and London. Especially in the north and the east, A.H. Wheeler and Company took off. It not only had the exclusive rights to run bookstalls on railway platforms, it also became the sole agency for issuing advertisements on behalf of the railways across most of India. T.K. Banerjee joined the firm in 1899, and after World War I became a partner. Wheeler and Company added vernacular books and journals to its product line. Eventually, Moreau retired and returned to England. Interestingly, his house in Brighton was named Fairlie Place, and was the headquarters of the EIRC. When Moreau retired, the Banerjee family

Anu Kumar, 23 April 2016, http://scroll.in/article/750419/the-many-lives-of-the-mysterious-emile-edouard-moreau-founder-of-ah-wheeler-and

[97] *Ibid.*

took over the equity of A.H. Wheeler. Let us make that exclusive rights privilege a little bit more precise. A.H. Wheeler and Company didn't have an exclusive monopoly throughout India—understandable, because of the fragmented way in which the railways developed. It had a monopoly everywhere but for what later became the Southern Railways and parts of the South Central Railway. This monopoly was eventually scrapped in 2004.

Another 1888 Kipling publication

In the south, there was Higginbotham's, which too had a monopoly till 2004. Higginbotham's was based in Chennai. Abel Joshua Higginbotham was reportedly a stowaway on a ship. On being discovered by the angry captain, he was dumped in Madras. Eventually, Higginbotham bought the stock of the Wesleyan Book Shop, a book store in Madras that wasn't doing too well, and this became Higginbotham's on Mount Road. This was in 1843. By 1859, Higginbotham's was the most important bookshop throughout the south. In 1859, Sir Charles Trevelyan, who was the Governor of Madras, said to Lord Macaulay in one of his letters: 'Among the many elusive and indescribable charms of life in Madras City, is the existence of my favourite book shop "Higginbotham's" on Mount Road. In this bookshop I can see beautiful editions of the works of Socrates, Plato, Euripides, Aristophanes, Pindar, Horace, Petrarch, Tasso, Camoyens, Calderon and Racine. I can get the latest editions of Victor Hugo, the great French novelist. Amongst the German writers, I can have Schiller and Goethe. Altogether a delightful place for the casual browser and a serious book lover.'[98]

When the Prince of Wales (the future Edward VII) visited India in 1875, Higginbotham's became 'booksellers to his Royal Highness', an honour that no other bookseller in India ever received. In 1888–89, Abel Joshua Higginbotham would go on to become the Sheriff of Madras. When he died in 1891, his son took over the business. (That ownership would pass into Indian hands in 1945.) Higginbotham's wasn't purely into selling books. It also ventured into publishing. For our purposes, what is important is that Higginbotham's had the monopoly for operating bookstalls in all railway stations that were under the South Indian Railway and the Southern Mahratta Railway.

---

[98] 'Deathless "Humanity in Print" in South India', V. Sundaram, *News Today*, 22 September 2005.

As mentioned earlier in this chapter, by the end of the nineteenth century, state ownership had come to predominate. But it was an extremely complicated regime.

At the dawn of the 20th Century, nearly fifty years after the first Railway train steamed out of Bori Bunder, there were thirty three separate Railway Administrations in India, operating over 41,000 route kilometres of Railway lines. Of these, four were worked by Government, five by the erstwhile Indian States, and the remaining 24 by private Railway Companies. The Non-Government Railways—i. e., other than the four owned and directly worked by the Government—operated under varying degrees of Government supervision. Their regulation and control vested in the Railway Branch of the Public Works Department of the Government of India. The Department was headed by an officer of the Indian Civil Service who was a member of the Viceroy and Governor General's Executive Council . . . The accounting and auditing functions for the whole Department, including the Railway Branch, were combined in the Accountant General, Public Works Department . . . In October 1901, the Secretary of State for India in Council appointed Sir Thomas Robertson, C.V.O., as Special Commissioner for Indian Railways to enquire into and report on the administration and working of the Indian Railways. In his report (1903), Sir Thomas recommended setting up of a Railway Board consisting of a President or Chief Commissioner, and two other Commissioners all of whom should have a practical knowledge of Railway matters and should be 'men of high railway standing' . . . As a consequence of these recommendations, it was decided early in 1905 to abolish the Railway Branch of the Public Works Department and to transfer the control of the Railway systems to a Railway Board consisting of a Chairman and two Members.[99]

The substantive bit was about the transfer of Indian railways from the public works department of the government of India to the Railway Board. This doesn't mean the other Robertson recommendations were accepted. For instance, Robertson recommended that the operation of state-managed lines should be handed back to private companies. Unhappy with some of the Robertson recommendations, the government appointed the Mackay Committee (the official title of the committee was 'Committee on Indian Railway Finance and Administration').[100] Appointed in 1904, the Mackay Committee submitted its report in 1908.

Meanwhile, the Railway Board was set up through the Indian Railway Boards Act of 1905. The resolution of 18 February 1905 explains what the Railway Board was expected to do.[101]

There are two distinct classes of duties with which the new authority will have to deal. The first is

[99] http://www.indianrailways.gov.in/railwayboard/uploads/codesmanual/irfc1/chapter%20-%201%20(R).pdf

[100] See, Kerr (1995).

[101] http://rti.railnet.gov.in/RTI_4_1/RTI_4_1/OM_item%201.pdf

deliberative and includes the preparation of the railway programme and the greater questions of railway policy and financial affecting all lines. The ultimate decision on such questions must of necessity rest with the government of India. The second class of duties is administrative, and includes such matters as construction of new lines by State Agency, the carrying out of new works on open lines,[102] the improvement of railway management with regard both to economy and public convenience, the arrangement for thorough traffic, and the settlement of dispute between railways. It is in respect to these duties that the greatest advantage in the establishment of an authority outside the Government of India is looked for.

The objectives were multiple and conflicting, and would plague the railways in the future. At that time, the Railway Board's office was in Shimla, not Delhi. The heritage building in which the office was housed was constructed in 1896–97 as the 'Public Works Department Secretariat Offices', the construction being carried out by the firm Richardson and Cruddas. When the Railway Board was set up, it was housed, together with the department of commerce, in this building. With the Railway Board having moved to Delhi, the building now houses other government offices.

---

[102] The term 'open line' is used quite a lot in the railways. In this 1905 context, it is important to pin down what it meant. It meant a line that is already open and running, as opposed to a new line being constructed.

**The old Railway Board
building, Shimla**

*Courtesy www.victorianweb.org by
Jacqueline Banerjee*

At the end of this chapter, we thought it would be in order
to mention Durgacharan Ray. In 1880, he published a
longish story, a bit like a travelogue, in Bengali.[103] This
was titled *Debganer Martye Agaman* (The Gods Come to
Earth). The gods, that is, Brahma, Indra and Varuna,
visit earth. More specifically, they visit Calcutta, then the
capital of India. The purpose of the visit is to take stock of
the effects of British rule in India. This taking stock also
involved the railways, since they took a train to Calcutta
and were barred from entering the waiting room at the
railway station because the definition of 'gentlemen', who
were entitled to use the waiting room, did not apply to
the non-British, gods or otherwise. But the gods were so
impressed that they resolved to replicate many of these
marvels, including the railways, in heaven.

---

[103] Dey's Publishing, Calcutta, reprinted this in 1984.

5

THE 20TH CENTURY: THE RAILWAY BOARD AND BEYOND

We will begin this chapter with a very long quotation from an 'essay' written by N.G. Priestley, the first Secretary of the Railway Board.[104] Written in 1905, these selected quotations are useful because they provide a very good thumbnail sketch of where the railways stood at the turn of the century.

> Lord Dalhousie in 1853 urged the importance of a speedy and wide introduction of railway communications throughout India; he pointed out the great social, political, and commercial advantages of constructing railways between the chief cities; and he specially recommended that, in the first instance, a system of trunk lines should be formed, connecting

---

[104] Collected by the authors from Railway archives.

the interior of each Presidency with its principal port and the several Presidencies with each other.

The trunk lines proposed were: a line from Calcutta to Lahore; a line from Bombay to some point in Hindustan, or alternatively a line by the Narbada valley to meet at some point the line from Calcutta to Lahore; a line uniting Bombay and Madras; and a line from Madras to the Malabar coast.

The Court of Directors accepted the general plan proposed; and by the end of 1859 eight companies had been formed for the construction of nearly 5,000 miles of line, with a capital under guarantee of pound 52,500,000 sterling. Thus was laid the foundation of the system of railways now existing in India, which amounted on June 30, 1905, to 28,054 miles, and which, radiating from the ports of Calcutta, Bombay, Madras, Karachi, Chittagong, and Rangoon, literally extends throughout the length and breadth of India, and connects, or is in process of connecting, every city of any importance and every Province. A few trunk lines, notably the Bombay-Sind, the Bengal-Assam, the Assam-Burma, the north and south broad-gauge connections, and the linking up of the metre-gauge systems of Northern, Central, and Southern India, still remain to be constructed; some large tracts of country have not yet been opened up by railways; and many railways require feeder lines.

All these projects are now being taken in hand, in the order of their importance, as funds become available. During the six years ending 1905, the length opened for traffic was 6,014 miles, or considerably more than was added during any similar period. But even at this rate the development of railway communications is regarded by many as not so rapid as the circumstances of the country require and would justify. The hindrance to a quicker expansion has been mainly financial.

All the original applicants for concessions for the financing of railways demanded that a minimum return should be guaranteed by the Government on their capital; and as companies could not be promoted without this condition, a guarantee of 5 per cent, was eventually agreed to, coupled with the free grant of all land needed. In return, the companies were required to share surplus profits half-yearly with the Government after the guaranteed interest for the half-year had been met, exchange for the remittance of interest charges being reckoned at 22d. to the rupee; to sell their railways to the Government after 25 years, at a rate specified; and to permit the Government to exercise the closest control over all expenditure and over the management and working of the line. These conditions would have been favourable to the Government if the guarantees had earned. But all expectations in regard to profits were destroyed by the heavy outlay on the construction of the lines.

The science of construction had not reached a high state of development, and the general idea seemed to have been that railways could not be efficiently managed unless they were built to a standard which was far in excess of the needs of the time. There were no engineers in India qualified to construct railways, and men had to be procured from England who were necessarily ignorant of the country, its conditions, and its language. They had neither experience of India, nor history to guide them; and there was no organization of labour in existence for works of such magnitude. They had, consequently, to learn by practical experiment what to avoid and what to adopt.

The Government officers in India on whom fell the duty of criticism of schemes, approval of works, and general control over expenditure, were themselves unfamiliar with railway practice. They could not therefore render any professional assistance to the engineers; and their supervision and control was carried to a degree of minuteness, which led to the appointment of a Committee of the House of Commons in 1857-8 to inquire into the delays alleged to have occurred in the construction of Indian railways.

The difficulties were reflected in the work done. The standard of construction was far higher than required for the conditions of the country, or for the actual work, which the railways were designed to perform. Conveniences were provided which, while in themselves desirable, were unnecessary for the safe or efficient operation of the railway; and the experimental lines were built with a double track, the necessity for which did not arise till a generation later. A further increase in the cost of construction was caused by alterations in the routes after work had been actually commenced. The outbreak of the Mutiny in 1857 added to the burden, by throwing everything into confusion and causing the suspension of all work for a time. Consequently, the earnings, which might have been sufficient to pay interest charges on a reasonable expenditure, proved inadequate to meet the guarantee on the outlay actually incurred, and Government had to make good the deficit.

By 1879, the continued fall in the gold value of silver and the series of famines between 1874 and 1878 had so disturbed the financial position of the Government, that the question of providing funds for the construction of railways in India was referred to a Committee of the House of Commons. This Committee advised that the total to be borrowed in any year for both railway and irrigation projects should be limited to the amount which could be raised in India without unduly depressing the market: a total that was estimated at 2 & 1/2 crores, of which 2 crores was assigned to railways. It was obvious that not much progress could be made with so small an outlay, and the Government again endeavoured to attract unaided private enterprise, but the results were not encouraging. Four companies were promoted: namely, the Nilgiri, the Delhi–Kalka, the Bengal Central, and the Bengal and

North-Western Railways. The first of these became bankrupt, the second and third eventually received a guarantee, and the Tirhut State Railway had to be leased to the fourth. Native States were also invited to undertake the construction of railways in their territory independently of Government aid, and a commencement was made with the Nizam's State Railway, a length of 330 miles.

As exchange continued to fall and had begun to affect seriously the finances of India, it became necessary for the Government to avoid increasing their gold liabilities, which terms in necessarily rose so long as the construction of railways by state agency continued; and in 1893 another attempt was made to work through companies. But as a guarantee involved the same gold liability, a subsidy was offered instead. This took the form of a rebate or payment from the gross earnings of the main line from traffic inter changed with the company's line, so that the total profits of the company should yield a dividend of 4 per cent. The rebate was, however, limited to 10 per cent, of the gross earnings from such traffic. The only companies promoted under these conditions were the Ahmadabad-Parantij, the South Bihar, and the Southern Punjab, though in the case only of the first, were the terms adhered to strictly. The Barsi Light Railway, which was promoted at the same time, received no assistance from the Government except free land. These conditions were found to be insufficiently attractive and the terms were revised in 1896. Companies were now offered either an absolute guarantee of 3 per cent., with a share of surplus profits, or a rebate up to the full extent of the main line's net earnings in supplement of their own net earnings, the total being limited to 3 & ½ per cent, on the capital outlay.

With the inclusion of all railways, for which the Government was financially responsible, in the programme, the capital budget allotments necessarily required to be increased. An improvement in exchange, in consequence of the closing of the mints to the free coinage of silver, made this possible, but a severe famine in Gujarat and the Deccan in 1899-1900 again caused expenditure on railways to be curtailed. The position had now become acute. The development in both passenger and goods traffic required more rolling stock, larger stations and goods sheds, additional sidings and stations, and sometimes duplication of the permanent way. The increasing demand for a faster and better train service necessitated expenditure on interlocking plant and automatic brakes, if the safety of the travelling public was to receive due consideration. With a limited and varying programme, either the construction of new lines had to be stopped or work on open lines had to be deferred. A middle course was taken, and neither one nor the other received all the funds needed. The difficulties of the railways in properly conducting their business finally became so great that it was decided in 1901 to adopt the principle of regarding the needs of open lines to meet their growing traffic as a first charge upon the funds available; next in order provision is made for the steady and early completion of lines in progress, preference being given to companies, lines over those under construction by the agency of the state; and after these needs have been met, the claims of new lines are considered.

Notwithstanding these difficulties Government had succeeded in providing India, up to the end of June, 1905, with 28,054 miles of railway at a cost of 359 crores of rupees or 240,000,000 sterling. Of this total, 14,705 miles have been constructed by the state, 6,935 under the guarantee system, 3,574 by Native States, 1,459 by companies with assistance in some form or other but without a guarantee, 1,307 by companies without assistance other than free land, and 74 by foreign Governments. Some of the lines included under the head 'guaranteed' are shown in the accounts as state lines, though they were originally promoted under a guarantee, or subsequently received one. Of the original lines constructed under a guarantee, only two were worked in 1905 under their old contracts: the Bombay, Baroda, and Central India, which was acquired by the state at the end of that year; and the Madras Railway, the contract of which is terminable in 1907.

Nevertheless, it had long been felt that the organization of a Government secretariat was hardly

qualified to give to the railway administration of
so vast a continent as India the elasticity that was
desirable, or to ensure sufficient attention being paid
to the commercial aspects of railway policy. Further,
the subordination of the Public Works Department
to a Member of Council of the Civil Service did
not provide adequately for the exercise of expert
authority in the final decisions of Government. For
many years a change of system had been advocated.
It was reserved for Lord Curzon's Government to
carry this into effect. Before proceeding to formulate
any definite scheme, they sought the services of an
English railway expert, Mr. Thomas Robertson,
who spent the winters of 1901 and 1902 in studying
the railways of India, and the summer of 1902 in
studying the methods adopted in America. He then
submitted a report, in which he recommended
that the existing system should be replaced by a
Railway Board, consisting of a chairman and two
members with a secretary, on the ground that for
the proper administration of railways a small body
of practical business men was needed, to whom
should be entrusted full authority to manage
them on commercial principles, and who should
be freed from non-essential restrictions and
needlessly inelastic rules. He further submitted
recommendations covering almost every aspect
of railway administration, some of which are in
course of being carried into effect. The Railway
Board was formally constituted in March, 1905. It

has been placed outside of, but subordinate to, the Government of India.

The duties assigned to the Railway Board are of two kinds. Its deliberative functions include the preparation of the railway programme of expenditure and the discussion of the greater questions of railway policy and economy affecting all lines, the final authority for decisions in regard to which is still retained by the Government of India. Its administrative duties include the construction of new lines by state agency, the carrying out of new works on open lines, the improvement of railway management with regard to both economy and public convenience, the arrangements for through traffic, the settlement of disputes between lines, the control and promotion of the staff on state lines, and the general supervision over the working and expenditure of companies' lines. The final authority in regard to these administrative duties has been delegated, subject to restrictions, to the Railway Board.

When the idea of constructing railways in India was first started, it was considered that there would be little passenger traffic on account of the poverty of the people, and that the chief business would be derived from goods. It was not realized how important a part pilgrimages to the numerous sacred shrines and rivers all over India play in the daily life of the population. Before railways were open pilgrimages occupied months and absorbed the savings of a lifetime. A trip to Puri or Hardwar, or any other of the popular Hindu shrines, is no longer a formidable undertaking. The cost is comparatively trifling, and the journey involves an absence from home of only a few days. No religious festival is now held without bringing, often from very long distances, thousands of devotees to the several shrines. Even Mecca has been brought within easier reach of the faithful; and large numbers of Muhammadans, not only from India but also from Central Asia, now undertake the pilgrimage, which before was possible only for the wealthy. Another factor overlooked was that cheap, easy, and quick communications would enable the surplus population in congested areas to move to the more sparsely populated parts of the country, where labour alone was needed to make the soil yield bountiful harvests.

In a country which is almost entirely agricultural, and with distances so great as in India, the principal traffic of railways must necessarily be in goods. Before railways were made, the cultivator derived little benefit from an abundant harvest. His markets were confined to a small area; and if the supply was greater than the demand, as it would be in a good season, prices fell, and he was deprived of the profits from the larger yield and often found it more economical to leave part of his crop uncut. Railways have altered these conditions. The improvement in communications has equalized prices in the case of agricultural produce within reasonable distance from a railway. When harvests are abundant, food-stuffs no longer rot for want of buyers, since the farmer has access to all the markets of the world. The development in goods traffic has consequently been even more marked than in the case of passenger traffic. The total quantity of goods carried in 1904 was 52,000,000 tons, and the income derived from it was 25 crores, the average rate charged per ton per mile being 5-39 pies (or 0-46 of a penny). The traffic consists chiefly of grain and seeds (12,361,000 tons), coal (9,397,000 tons), cotton (1,584,000 tons), jute (1,500,000 tons), salt (1,647,000 tons), sugar (447,000 tons), and timber (1,250,000 tons). All this traffic was in country produce. A large part of the grain and seeds, cotton, and jute is exported; but the rest remains in the country, and the extent to which it circulates between different places may be judged by the fact that the distance each ton of goods was carried, reckoning the distance travelled over each railway as a separate journey, averaged 172 miles. The greatest development in recent years has been in the coal traffic. The principal collieries are situated in Bengal, and they are practically the only local source of supply for all Northern, Western, and Central India. For some time movement was prevented by high rates, and these regions found it cheaper to import from England; but the reductions made in recent years have caused the almost complete displacement of English coal by Indian. Except in the neighbourhood of the collieries, coal is still too expensive for domestic use by the natives, but further large reductions in the rates for coal are in contemplation.

The passenger-versus-freight comparison was extremely important, not just today, but even at that time. In the academic literature, a recent paper explored the impact of the railways in a cross-country and comparative perspective.[105] It is simplest to state the findings in the words of the authors:

It is widely recognized that railways were one of the most important drivers of economic growth in the 19th and 20th century, but it is less recognized that railways had a different impact across countries. In this paper, we first estimate the growth impact of Indian railways, one of the largest networks in the world circa 1900. Then, we show railways made a smaller contribution to income per-capita growth in India compared to the most dynamic Latin American economies between 1860 and 1912. The smaller contribution in India is related to four factors: (1) the smaller size of railway freight revenues in the Indian economy, (2) the higher elasticity of demand for freight services, (3) lower wages, and (4) higher fares. Our results suggest large disruptive technologies such

[105] 'The Growth Contribution of Colonial Indian Railways in Comparative Perspective,' Dan Bogart, Latika Chaudhury and Alfsonso Herranz-Loncan, February 2015, http://www.socsci.uci.edu/~dbogart/growthcontributionDraft,%20Feb2015.pdf

as railways and other communication technologies can generate huge resources savings, but may not have large growth impacts.

Reactions, both positive and negative, came also from the passenger perspective, and understandably so. Madhav Rao (1828–91) was successively chief minister of the princely states of Travancore, Indore and Baroda. He wrote in 1885: 'What a glorious change the railway has made in long and old neglected India! In passing from the banks of the Tambrapruny to those of the Ganges, what varied scenes, what successive nationalities and languages flit across the view! *Tamil, Telugu, Canarese, Marathi, Guzerathi, Hindustani, Bengali*—population which had been isolated for unmeasured ages, now easily mingled in civilized confusion. In my various long journeys it repeatedly struck me that if India is to become a homogenous nation, and is to ever achieve solidarity, it must be by means of the Railways as means of transport, and by means of the English language as a medium of communication.'[106]

This was one perspective, but there was another too. That second perspective comes from Mahatma Gandhi's *Hind Swaraj*, and was originally written in Gujarati in 1908.[107] For greater understanding, the book/monograph was written in the form of a dialogue between the Reader

[106] Quoted in Ian Kerr, *Engines of Change, op. cit.*

[107] *Hind Swaraj or Indian Home Rule*, M.K. Gandhi, http://www.mkgandhi.org/ebks/hind_swaraj.pdf

(the general Indian) and the Editor (Gandhiji). Since the Reader's comments are the standard ones about the benefits the railways brought, we will only quote the Editor's responses.

> It must be manifest to you that, but for the railways, the English could not have such a hold on India as they have. The railways, too, have spread the bubonic plague. Without them, the masses could not move from place to place. They are the carriers of plague germs. Formerly we had natural segregation. Railways have also increased the frequency of famines because, owing to facility of means of locomotion, people sell out their grain and it is sent to the dearest markets. People become careless and so the pressure of famine increases. Railways accentuate the evil nature of man: Bad men fulfil their evil designs with greater rapidity. The holy places of India have become unholy. Formerly, people went to these places with very great difficulty. Generally, therefore, only the real devotees visited such places. Nowadays rogues visit them in order to practice their roguery . . . Good travels at a snail's pace—it can, therefore, have little to do with the railways. Those who want to do good are not selfish, they are not in a hurry, they know that to impregnate people with good requires a long time. But evil has wings. To build a house takes time. Its destruction takes none. So the railways can become a distributing agency for the evil one only. It may be a debatable matter whether railways spread famines,

but it is beyond dispute that they propagate evil . . .
The English have taught us that we were not one
nation before and that it will require centuries before
we become one nation. This is without foundation.
We were one nation before they came to India. One
thought inspired us. Our mode of life was the same.
It was because we were one nation that they were
able to establish one kingdom. Subsequently they
divided us . . . I do not wish to suggest that because
we were one nation we had no differences, but it is
submitted that our leading men travelled throughout
India either on foot or in bullock-carts. They learned
one another's languages and there was no aloofness
between them. What do you think could have been
the intention of those farseeing ancestors of ours
who established Setubandha (Rameshwar) in the
South, Jagannath in the East and Hardwar in the
North as places of pilgrimage? You will admit they
were no fools. They knew that worship of God could
have been performed just as well at home. They
taught us that those whose hearts were aglow with
righteousness had the Ganges in their own homes.
But they saw that India was one undivided land so
made by nature. They, therefore, argued that it must
be one nation. Arguing thus, they established holy
places in various parts of India, and fired the people
with an idea of nationality in a manner unknown
in other parts of the world. And we Indians are
one as no two Englishmen are. Only you and I and
others who consider ourselves civilized and superior

persons imagine that we are many nations. It was after the advent of railways that we began to believe in distinctions, and you are at liberty now to say that it is through the railways that we are beginning to abolish those distinctions. An opium-eater may argue the advantage of opium-eating from the fact that he began to understand the evil of the opium habit after having eaten it. I would ask you to consider well what I had said on the railways.

The more important nationalist point was the segregation the railways brought about—Indians travelling in third class carriages, the discrimination they faced and the lack of Indianization within the railways. We alluded to bits of this in the preceding chapter, all reminiscent of Gandhiji's experiences in South Africa. There is more than one anecdote about this.[108] Justice Nanabhai Haridas was the first Indian judge of the Bombay High Court. In 1885, he was travelling from Bombay to Surat with his son. There was only one first class compartment, and this was occupied by Captain Loch and his wife. Though there were two empty seats, Captain Loch objected to Justice Haridas and his son being allowed to travel in the first class compartment. The stationmaster responded that nothing could be done about this since the compartment hadn't

[108] See, *Blood, Iron, and Gold: How the Railways Transformed the World*, Christian Wolmar, Atlantic Books, 2009. Wolmar incorrectly describes Sir Ashutosh Mukherjee as the first Chief Justice of Calcutta High Court. He was several things, and a trained lawyer, but never a judge.

been reserved. At this, Captain Loch paid and reserved
the entire compartment. Justice Haridas and his son had
no option but to travel in second class. The well-known
Bengali educator Sir Ashutosh Mukherjee was once
travelling in a first class compartment and went to sleep.
When he woke up, he discovered that his sandals were
missing. His fellow passenger was a British plantation
owner, who was unhappy at the prospect of travelling with
an Indian. Unable to do anything about it, he took the
opportunity of Sir Mukherjee going to sleep to fling his
sandals out of the window. Subsequently, when the British
plantation owner made the mistake of going to sleep and
Sir Mukherjee had woken up and discovered his sandals
missing, Sir Mukherjee flung the British gentleman's
jacket out of the window. When the plantation owner woke
up and inquired about his jacket, Ashutosh Mukherjee
retorted, 'Your coat has gone to fetch my slippers.'

Courtesy National Rail Museum, Delhi

Mahatma Gandhi in 1917

Courtesy National Rail Museum, Delhi

Third class travel, date not known

There were several reasons why Gandhiji took to travelling by third class. In 1917, while in Ranchi, he authored an essay on what it was like to travel by third class.[109] This is so vivid a description that it deserves to be quoted from at length.

> On the 12th instant I booked at Bombay for Madras by the mail train and paid Rs.13-9. It was labelled to carry 22 passengers. These could only have seating accommodation. There were no bunks in this carriage whereon passengers could lie with any degree of safety or comfort. There were two nights to be passed in this train before reaching Madras. If

---

[109] 'Third Class in Indian Railways', M.K. Gandhi. This essay, together with some others, which had nothing to do with the railways, was published in a collection with the same title, *Third Class in Indian Railways*, http://in.okfn.org/files/2013/07/Third-class-in-Indian-railways.pdf

not more than 22 passengers found their way into my carriage before we reached Poona, it was because the bolder ones kept the others at bay. With the exception of two or three insistent passengers, all had to find their sleep being seated all the time. After reaching Raichur the pressure became unbearable. The rush of passengers could not be stayed. The fighters among us found the task almost beyond them. The guards or other railway servants came in only to push in more passengers. A defiant Memon merchant protested against this packing of passengers like sardines. In vain did he say that this was his fifth night on the train. The guard insulted him and referred him to the management at the terminus. There were during this night as many as 35 passengers in the carriage during the greater part of it. Some lay on the floor in the midst of dirt and some had to keep standing. A free fight was, at one time, avoided only by the intervention of some of the older passengers who did not want to add to the discomfort by an exhibition of temper . . . On the way passengers got for tea tannin water with filthy sugar and a whitish looking liquid mis-called milk which gave this water a muddy appearance. I can vouch for the appearance, but I cite the testimony of the passengers as to the taste . . . Not during the whole of the journey was the compartment once swept or cleaned. The result was that every time you walked on the floor or rather cut your way through the passengers seated on the floor, you waded through dirt . . . The closet was also not cleaned during the journey and there was no water in the water tank . . . Refreshments sold to the passengers were dirty-looking, handed by dirtier hands, coming out of filthy receptacles and weighed in equally unattractive scales. These were previously sampled by millions of flies. I asked some of the passengers who went in for these dainties to give their opinion. Many of them used choice expressions as to the quality but were satisfied to state that they were helpless in the matter; they had to take things as they came . . . To this compartment there was a closet falsely so called. It was designed as a European closet but could hardly be used as such. There was a pipe in it but no water, and I say without fear of challenge that it was pestilentially dirty . . . The compartment itself was evil looking. Dirt was lying thick upon the wood work and I do not know that it had ever seen soap or water . . . The compartment had an exceptional assortment of passengers. There were three stalwart Punjabi Mahomedans, two refined Tamilians and two Mahomedan merchants who joined us later. The merchants related the bribes they had to give to procure comfort. One of the Punjabis had already travelled three nights and was weary and fatigued. But he could not stretch himself. He said he had sat the whole day at the Central Station watching passengers giving bribe to procure their tickets. Another said he had himself to pay Rs. 5 before he could get his ticket and his seat . . . But a third-class traveller is dumb and helpless. He does not want to complain even though to go to these places may be to court death. I know passengers who fast while they are travelling just in order to lessen the misery of their life in the trains. At Sonepur flies having failed, wasps have come forth to warn the public and the authorities, but yet to no purpose. At the Imperial Capital a certain third class booking-office is a Black-Hole fit only to be destroyed . . . Compare the lot of the first class passengers with that of the third class. In the Madras case the first class fare is over five times as much as the third class fare. Does the third class passenger get one-fifth, even one-tenth, of the comforts of his first class fellow? It is but simple justice to claim that some relative proportion be observed between the cost and comfort . . . It is a known fact that the third class traffic pays for the ever-increasing luxuries of first and second class travelling. Surely a third class passenger is entitled at least to the bare necessities of life . . . Among the many suggestions that can be made for dealing with the evil here described, I would respectfully include this: let the people in high places, the Viceroy, the Commander-in-Chief, the Rajas, Maharajas, the Imperial Councillors and others, who generally travel in superior classes, without previous warning, go through the experiences now and then of third class travelling. We would then soon see a remarkable change in the conditions of third class travelling and the uncomplaining millions will get some return for the fares they pay under the expectation of being carried from place to place with ordinary creature comforts.

Even if he didn't desire it, Gandhiji was a celebrity, with privileged status. A few years later, in 1921, he was due to visit Assam, to address a non-cooperation meeting in Jorhat. He was on a special train run by Jorhat Provincial Railway, which would later connect to the Assam Bengal Railway train to Dibrugarh. In the middle of the night, this special train rammed against a goods train that was running along the same track. In the process, the coach in which Gandhiji was travelling got detached, and the rest of the train chugged along on its journey. It was only later that it was discovered that Gandhiji had been left behind. The horrified guard and engine driver brought the train back and discovered Gandhiji was fine. Gandhiji laughed and remarked that he had despaired of the train ever coming back for him.

These days, with the exception of the Rajdhanis and the Shatabdis, most trains are identified by numbers. In those initial years of development of the railways, that wasn't the case. We have already mentioned the names of some of the famous locomotives. Once upon a time, all locomotives were christened. That gave them character. Trains also possessed names, and some of the famous trains had iconic value. The first such train was clearly the Punjab Mail, introduced between Ballard Pier (later from Victoria Terminus) and Peshawar (later to Firozpur) by GIPR in 1912. On some days, this had mail connections with P&O steamships. Indeed, that's how the Punjab Mail originally started. On those days, it operated as Punjab

Limited and operated from Ballard Pier (Mole Station) to Peshawar, covering a distance of almost 2500 km in forty-seven hours at a very respectable speed of fifty-three km per hour. Initially, there were six compartments—three for passengers and three for postal goods and mail. All three passenger compartments were first class, with two berths in each cabin. The entire train cost Rs 8,94,000 to construct. Its carriages were made out of special Burma teak.[110] When it started to run on every day of the week, the Punjab Limited became the Punjab Mail, and for a very long time was the fastest train in India. In the initial years, it was an extremely prestigious train, and that it was purely first class gave it exclusivity. The Punjab Mail was 'degraded' with the addition of third class carriages in the 1930s, second class passengers and 'servants' having been permitted earlier.

Courtesy IRFCA by Sentil Kumar

Great Indian Peninsula Railway.
—
ROYAL MAIL ROUTE.
—
Three Weekly Limited Expresses, conveying the English Mail, leave Bombay about four hours after arrival of the Inward P. & O. Mail Steamer.

1. To Cawnpore, Lucknow, Agra, Delhi, the Punjab, and Peshawar.
2. To Calcutta *via* Jubbulpore.
3. To Madras *via* Raichur.

Intending passengers can book at the P. & O. Offices in London or on Board and are landed with their luggage from the steamer by special launch. Bogie Carriages fitted with Electric Lights and Fans and Restaurant Car Service throughout the journey. Ordinary first class fares charged.

A board listing GIPR mail services, including the Punjab Mail

---

[110] http://www.irfca.org/~shankie/famoustrains/famtrainpunjmail.htm

Courtesy IRFCA by Sentil Kumar

THE PUNJAB ROYAL MAIL EXPRESS.

Through carriages between Bombay and Agra, Delhi, Kalka (for Simla), and the Punjab.

Fares from Bombay.

Station		H. M.	I Rs. a. p.	II Rs. a. p.	Servants. Rs. a. p.	Station		H. M.
Bombay	.. dep.	7-15 p.m.				Peshawar	dep.	6-54 a.m.
Manmad	.. "	0-49 a.m.	15 3 0	7 10 0	2 9 0	Rawalpindi	"	11-44 a.m.
Bhusaval	.. "	3-53 a.m.	25 14 0	12 15 0	4 5 0	Lahore	"	9-35 p.m.
Itarsi	.. "	8-50 a.m.	38 6 0	19 3 0	7 4 0	Simla	"	6-0 p.m.
Bina	.. "	1-5 p.m.	47 5 0	23 11 0	9 8 0	Umballa	"	3-55 a.m.
Jhansi	.. "	3-43 p.m.	53 4 0	26 10 0	11 0 0	Delhi	"	8-0 a.m.
Agra	.. "	8-5 p.m.	61 9 0	30 13 0	8 4 0	Muttra	"	10-15 a.m.
Muttra	.. "	8-57 p.m.	57 13 0	28 15 0	7 9 0	Agra	"	11-9 a.m.
Delhi	.. "	11-25 p.m.	66 4 0	33 3 0	8 12 0	Jhansi	"	3-58 p.m.
Umballa	.. "	3-17 a.m.	77 13 0	38 15 0	10 6 0	Bina	"	6-35 p.m.
Simla	.. arr.	12-42 p.m.	103 5 0	52 11 0	14 11 0	Itarsi	"	10-49 p.m.
Lahore	.. dep.	11-54 a.m.	94 2 0	47 2 0	12 4 0	Bhusaval	"	3-24 a.m.
Rawalpindi	. .	6-51 p.m.	106 4 0	53 4 0	14 6 0	Manmad	"	6-46 a.m.
Peshawar	.. arr.	11-18 p.m.	113 0 0	56 10 0	15 10 0	Bombay	arr.	12-35 p.m.

A through carriage also runs daily by this train between Jhansi and Dehra Dun *via* Delhi, Ghaziabad, Meerut and Saharanpur.

Luxuriously equipped carriages fitted with Electric Lights and Fans, Restaurant Car Service. Conveys I and II Class passengers, and their servants only.

The Punjab Mail schedule

Later, the Punjab Mail was overshadowed by the Frontier Mail. There used to be a Mumbai–Peshawar Mail, which the BBCI replaced with the Frontier Mail in 1928. During the winter months, from September to December, the Frontier Mail connected with P&O steamships and therefore started from Ballard Pier (Mole Station). Consequently, the BBCI used the Bombay Port Railway tracks and also those of the GIPR before it moved on to its own lines. In the non-winter months, the train ended at Colaba. The GIPR and the BBCI competed over several milestones, such as which company would cross the Western Ghats first. They also competed over the Mumbai–Peshawar route, and once it was started, the Frontier Mail overtook the Punjab Mail. It was faster and more elitist. Initially, there were five coaches and a dining-cum-lounge car. The coaches had cooling systems that used blocks of ice. The Frontier Mail was known for its punctuality. It was said that a Rolex watch might let you down, but not the Frontier Mail. In August 1929, there was an instance when the train was fifteen minutes late, and this created an uproar, the driver being asked to explain the reason for this 'inexcusable' delay.[111] In 1936, Wadia Movietone decided to produce an action crime thriller directed by Homi Wadia. This starred 'Fearless Nadia' (Mary Ann Evans) and the setting for the murder mystery was a railway station. Unfortunately, the film was titled *Frontier Mail*. The BBCI objected, since the film showed a crashing train, that too, after the film company had been allowed to film on the BBCI trains.

Four weeks before *Miss Frontier Mail*'s release in May 1936, producer J.B.H. Wadia was contacted by an angry B.B. & C.I. Railway company official complaining that he had betrayed their trust. The company had allowed Wadia's crew to film on their trains and tracks. He had rewarded them with *Frontier Mail*, a film about the dangers of rail travel, starring India's top female box-office draw, Fearless Nadia. Advertising it throughout the country with a graphic image of a train crash, a misguided publicist had added: 'By kind permission of the B.B. & C.I. Railway Company'. Keen to appease the railway owners but ever the opportunist, J.B.H. Wadia immediately instigated a national newspaper campaign to find a new name for the film. Thousands of suggestions flooded in from the public, from amongst which the simple addition of 'Miss' to 'Frontier Mail' seemed least likely to cause complications for a completed film awaiting imminent

---

[111] http://www.irfca.org/~shankie/famoustrains/famtrainfrontier.htm

release.[112] Accordingly, the *Miss Frontier Mail* publicity booklet stated, 'We hereby inform the public that our Rail-Road Thriller, *Miss Frontier Mail*, has no connections whatsoever with the well-known "Frontier Mail" of the B.B. & C.I. Railway. It refers to the name of the heroine of the story and not to any train whatsoever in India.'

The iconic Frontier Mail now goes by the rather pedestrian-sounding name of the Golden Temple Mail.

The film must have been a success. In 1939, Wadia Movietone produced a film titled *Punjab Mail*, again starring Fearless Nadia; the GIPR does not seem to have objected. (There were no crashing trains in this one.) Wadia Movieteone also produced *Toofan Mail* in 1932, and *Toofan Express* in 1938, the former being a silent film. Once upon a time, Toofan Express used to be a great train between Delhi and Howrah (later extended to Sri Ganganagar), 7 UP and 8 DN. It is now called Udyan Abha Toofan Express, 13007/13008. Several people, even within Indian Railways, will tell you about a train called Toofan Mail. You may be surprised to know there never was such a train. Officially, it was always Toofan Express. There have been too many films titled *Jawab*, but can the reader remember Kanan Devi's song from the 1942 *Jawab*? 'Toofan Mail, *Duniya yeh duniya toofan mail*.' There was also a 1942 film called *Return of Toofan Mail*; it was the influence of Bollywood that reduced Toofan Express to Toofan Mail.

---

[112] 'Miss Frontier Mail: The Film That Mistook Its Star for a Train', Rosie Thomas, *Sarai Reader*, 2007, http://westminsterresearch. wmin.ac.uk/4710/1/Thomas_2007_final.pdf

Poster promoting the movie *Miss Frontier Mail*

The Mumbai–Pune Deccan Queen is the only train that has a birthday that is celebrated. This GIPR train was started on 1 June 1930. Originally, this was a train that only operated over the weekends. But in the 1940s it became a daily train. The Deccan Queen is the first train to have a 'Ladies Only' compartment; and the first to have a vestibule running throughout its length. It was also one of those rare trains that had never been hauled using steam traction. The traction has been electric, and in some rare instances, diesel. The Deccan Queen has sometimes been described as a train that catered to the Poona races, but that is probably not correct. Towards the end of the nineteenth century, the GIPR introduced special trains for the Poona races. At the time when the Deccan Queen was introduced, the Poona Mail used to take six hours to do the Mumbai–Pune stretch. The Deccan Queen brought it down to a remarkable two hours and forty-five minutes. This broke the record of three hours and twenty-six minutes, held by the GIPR's Poona race specials.

Courtesy IRFCA by John Lacey

An advertisement poster for the Deccan Queen

The Grand Trunk Express between Peshawar and Mangalore, introduced by the Madras and Southern Mahratta Railway in 1929, was another such long-distance train. The Flying Ranee that plied between Bombay Central and Surat, and operated by the BBCI, was another, though this was more a medium-distance train. This train was also known as the Flying Queen, although more accurately, that was its name in the 1930s. Starting as a weekend special, the train operated as the Flying Ranee between 1906 and 1914. Not much is known about that period. In 1937, it was reintroduced as the Flying Queen and operated under this name up to 1939. A description of that 1937 relaunch is available:[113]

> Mrs Sethna, wife of the District Superintendent Bulsar, who has taken a leading part in the inception and organization of the service, undertook the pleasant duty of naming the train before a large holiday crowd. Standing on a platform alongside the gigantic locomotive which was gaily decorated for the occasion, Mrs Sethna said: 'I name you Flying Ranee, Queen of the West Coast. May all your trips be safe and may all those who travel by you enjoy a happy and carefree holiday, and a safe and comfortable homeward journey.' This brief address was repeated in Gujarati, after which Mrs Sethna unveiled the name plaque on the engine's smoke-box door.

In the list of iconic trains, there are two more that merit mention. One was the Imperial Indian Mail, introduced in 1926 between Bombay and Calcutta, jointly introduced by the EIRC and GIPR. There was a multi-modal angle at both ends of its journey. At one end, passengers arrived by ship at Bombay's Ballard Pier, from London. They then caught the Imperial Indian Mail from Bombay to Howrah. At the other end, they boarded a steamer to Rangoon. The last one that must be mentioned is the Boat Mail. This was also multi-modal, because a train and steamer ferry service connected India with Ceylon (Sri Lanka). The initial route, in the nineteenth century, was from Madras to Tuticorin,

---

[113] http://www.irfca.org/~shankie/famoustrains/famtrainfranee.htm

from where there was a steamer service to Colombo. However, after the Pamban Bridge was constructed in 1914, the route changed to Madras–Dhanushkodi. From Dhanushkodi, there was a short ferry ride to Talaimannar and then a train ride from Talaimannar to Colombo. Much later, in 1964, a cyclone destroyed Dhanushkodi and the train. Dhanushkodi became a ghost town, and that was the end of the Boat Mail.

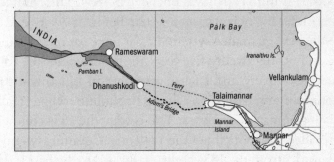

The Boat Mail route

We have moved into the 1920s. That can't be done without mentioning the Acworth Committee. As we have earlier said, by the end of the nineteenth century, the government of India started acquiring some of the older railways and also started railway construction of its own. This affected the government's budget and finances. Revenues from railways were considerable, and any volatility in these meant that government receipts declined.[114] At the

---

[114] The Acworth Committee and its recommendations have been discussed threadbare and we don't wish to repeat what is already known. See, for example, the discussion in *Indian Railways, Strategy for Reforms*, K.B. Verma, Foundation Books, 2015.

same time, when government receipts declined, capital expenditure on railways suffered. The trigger was the management contract with the EIRC. When that came up for renewal in 1920, the government appointed a committee under the chairmanship of William Mitchell Acworth. Its report was submitted in 1921.

A bit more specifically, though the EIRC was formed in 1845, it had signed a contract with the East India Company in 1849 that was amended in 1854. This contract was under the old guarantee system before it was tweaked to the new guarantee system. Leases were for ninety-nine years, but after twenty-five years, the government (the East India Company, and later government of India) had the option of purchasing everything (including rolling stock, plant and machinery) back. This is what the 1854 contract provided for, though not the 1849 one. Counting twenty-five years from the 1854 contract, this led to the East India Railway Company Purchase Act of 1879, a statute for the nationalization of railways. However, though ownership changed, the EIRC was allowed the franchise to operate the railway for fifty years. The EIRC's status changed from (1) to (4) and this was to be reviewed in 1919 (as that would mark fifty years of the signing of the franchise agreement in 1869).

William Acworth was quite a railway expert. He wrote several books on railways and railway economics. He lectured on railways at the London School of Economics. Across the world, he was a member of several commissions on railways. The Legislative Assembly of the government of India considered the recommendations of the Acworth

Committee in 1924. Most people only quote a particular section from the Acworth Committee Report. The Nehru Memorial Museum and Library (NMML) is probably one of the rare places where all volumes of the Acworth Committee Report are available. In this set, a specific section has been marked out in pencil. Sub-consciously, probably, everyone feels the urge to quote this.

> We do not think that the Indian railways can be modernized, improved and enlarged, so as to give to India the service of which it is in crying need at the moment, nor that the railways can yield to the Indian public the financial return which they are entitled to expect from so valuable a property, until the whole financial methods are radically reformed. And the essence of this reform is contained in two things: (1) the complete separation of the Railway Budget from the General Budget of the country, and its reconstruction in a form which frees a great commercial business from the trammels of a system which assumes that the concern goes out of business on each 1st of March and recommences *de novo* on the 1st of April; and (2) the emancipation of the railway management from the control of the Finance Department.

While that's fine, the Acworth Committee itself said it had twenty-four unanimous recommendations and another twenty-six divergent/supplementary recommendations. For example, it says, 'We suggest that there should be a less rigid regard than hitherto to the claims of seniority.' The importance of adhering to commercial accounting principles was also stressed. The recommendation of the separate Railway Budget was possibly the only recommendation[115] of the committee that got implemented. A financial commissioner for the Railways was appointed in 1923. Then, through the Separation Convention of 1924, railway finances were separated from general finances.

In 2012–13, as railway minister, Dinesh Trivedi gave us an interesting titbit of information in his Railway Budget speech:

> Madam Speaker, in the last eight months of my working as Railway Minister, I have received as many as 5741 requests. These include 476 requests for projects of new lines, doubling and gauge conversion or expediting their completion; 273 requests for construction of ROB/RUBs; 41 for

---

[115] Some of the other noteworthy recommendations of the Acworth Committee included:

a) Creation of a new 'Department of Communications' responsible for railways, ports and inland navigation, road transport, and posts & telegraph;

b) Presentation of accounts and statistics to be thoroughly overhauled and remodelled with the assistance of experts familiar with recent practice in other countries;

c) Establishment of Central and Local Railway Advisory Councils to enable the Indian public to have an adequate representation and voice in the management of the Railways; and that these councils should be established as soon as possible;

d) Reasonable general increase in Indian rates and fares;

e) Establishment of a rates tribunal to examine reasonableness of rates and facilities.

electrification; 48 for setting of manufacturing facilities; 646 requests for new trains; 303 for extension of trains; 214 for increasing the frequency of trains; another 811 for train stoppages; and about 3000 requests for miscellaneous areas such as transfers and postings of railway employees and passenger amenities etc.

If one goes by media reports, there will be no Railway Budget from 2017–18. That's the way the media puts it, but it is a bad way of explaining the change that is going to happen (if it does). Every organization has a budget, and so will the Indian Railways. What will be different is that a railway minister will no longer present this budget in Parliament through a speech. That separate presentation will not be required, legally and Constitutionally.

It is important to highlight the key drivers that led to the Acworth Committee recommending the separation of railway finances from the general finances of the government:

a) In the 1920s, the railways accounted for a dominant share of the economic activity in India. Revenues from the railways accounted for about 50 per cent of overall Government of India (GoI) revenues during that period, while the net revenues (excluding working expenses) accounted for about a third of GoI revenues.[116] In terms of the inter-modal passenger and freight transport market shares, the

---

[116] Acworth Committee findings (Clause 33 and Clause 90)

railways catered to the bulk of the transportation requirements in the country.

b) The allocations to the Railways, particularly for capital works, exhibited volatility, depending upon the general financial situation of the Government. For those years when GoI revenues were strained, capital allocation to railways suffered considerably. The following comment of the Acworth Committee is particularly noteworthy:

'34. Now, it is the prime duty of the Indian Chancellor of the Exchequer, the Finance Member of the Council, to balance his Budget. In times of bad harvests and bad trade receipts fall off. The Finance Member is constrained to economize. He cannot reduce the army or the civil services wholesale at short notice. He can and does curtail his appropriation to railways for renewals and betterment works. And he cuts down still more drastically expenditure on new works and extensions, even though they may be in process of execution . . .'

c) Besides the above, during a particular year when there were difficulties, sums already allocated to the railways were abruptly slashed and works in progress suspended, staff disbanded, and materials left lying around unused for an indefinite period. Further, due to the uncertainty in revenues, funds for railway works were, at times, allocated as late as in February or even March, to be spent by the end of March.[117]

d) The separation of the Railway Budget was therefore a means to provide full financial autonomy to Indian Railways and to protect its commercial business

---

[117] *Acworth Committee Report* (Clause 36)

character. This, in turn, was intended to ensure that Indian Railways stayed an empowered ecosystem that could fund its capital and operational and maintenance investment needs by itself, and at the same time provide a fair and a reasonable return to the government on its investments.[118]

As we stated earlier, that expression '*imperium in imperio*' was often used in connection with the Indian railways, and is sometimes used even today. It means 'empire within an empire'. Who first used it for the

---

[118] Quotation from the Commerce Member submitting the Separation Convention in 1924 to the Legislative Assembly:

'In the first place, as far as State Railways are concerned, we want to abolish altogether this system of programme revenue voted for a year. We want to establish a proper depreciation fund, a depreciation fund arranged in a scientific and intelligible manner. Secondly, we want to build up Railway reserves. We want to build them up in order that our finances may be more elastic, in order that we may have provision to equalize dividends. And generally, we want to introduce a system of finance which while maintaining unimpaired the centrality of this House and while ensuring to general revenues a fair return from their Railway property, will be more suited to the needs of a vast commercial undertaking. Finally, and most important of all, we want to establish the principle, that it is right and proper that the tax-payer, the State, should get a fair and stable return from the money it has spent on its Railways; but if you go further, if you take from the Railways more than that fair return, then you are indulging in a concealed way in one of the most vicious forms of taxation, namely a tax on transportation. One of the objects we have most at heart in putting these proposals before this House is to establish that principle.'
(Source:http://www.indianrailways.gov.in/railwayboard/uploads/codesmanual/ADMIN_FINANCE/AdminFinanceCh7_Data.htm)

railways? That doesn't seem to be very easy to answer.
In Parliamentary debates, it was used for the East India
Company in 1857.[119] Specifically for the railways, Lord
Salisbury is believed to have first used the expression,
towards the end of the 1870s. We believe the expression
was first used by 'an old Indian postmaster' named W.P.
Andrew, in a book published in 1848.[120] Though the
reference is a trifle indirect, he does seem to have had the
railways—that is, railway companies—in mind.

> There is much additional matter introduced in
> this impression, in connection with the statistics
> of India and other subjects having reference to the
> requirements of that country, for improved internal
> communication, or to its capabilities of emancipating
> itself from its primitive, rude, and most inefficient
> roads and conveyances, achieving by one mighty
> bound, what other nations have taken centuries
> to accomplish; and, profiting by the experience
> of Europe, selecting what has worked well in the
> several modes of railway administration, such a
> controlling power might be easily placed in the
> hands of the Government, without deadening the
> impulse which private enterprise alone can impart,
> and effectually prevent the springing up in India
> of an 'imperium in imperio', as has resulted in this

---

[119] http://www.victorianweb.org/history/empire/1857/bm7.html
[120] *Indian Railways and their probable results*, An Old Indian
Postmaster, T. G. Newby and Richardson, London, 1848.

country from the laxity or want of foresight on the part of the legislature, and the encroaching audacity of successful enterprise, placing the roads of this great country—the arteries of her vital energy and strength—in the hands of private individuals, with power to tax their fellow subjects, without appeal, to an amount equal to the revenues of a mighty Empire.

So far, we have not said anything about crime on the railways. As railway networks spread, they, understandably, provided new opportunities for crime—on trains, at stations and even in freight sheds. There was an Indian Police Commission in 1902–03 that made several comments about the railway police.[121]

There are no less than three different systems of railway police administration in operation at the present time. There are (1) The district system, under which the railway police form part of the force of each district through which the railway runs. This is in operation only in a part of the Central Provinces, and it is found necessary to allow some departure from it and to have a few officers with jurisdiction over the whole line. (2) The provincial system, under which there is a separate railway police for the province,

---

[121] http://bprd.nic.in/writereaddata/linkimages/2108898614-THE%20POLICE%20COMMISSION%20REPORT%201860.pdf

the jurisdiction being bounded by the limits of the province, irrespective of the limits of the railway administration. (3) The railway administration, without regard to provincial boundaries. It has been proposed that, as a development of this last-mentioned system, the railway police force should be made an Imperial establishment for the whole of India. The Commission are unable to accept this suggestion. The unit of police administration is the province, and a departure from this principle in the case of the railway police would greatly weaken the co-operation between that force and the district police, a co-operation which is admitted by all to be essential for efficiency in police work. It would also render impossible the connection between the railway police and the proposed provincial Criminal Investigation Departments, and would thus deprive the latter of a most valuable auxiliary staff. For the same reasons, the Commission are opposed to the Railway Administration system, for it involves a police force under one Local Government working within the jurisdiction of another, an arrangement which has been condemned by nearly all witnesses who have had experience of it, especially in Sind, though it is, not unnaturally, favoured by many railway officials, as they prefer to deal with a single set of police officers. The Commission readily admit that this is a great convenience, but they have no hesitation in saying that this advantage is far outweighed by the benefits obtained from adherence to the principle of provincial unity. That principle is maintained under the district system, but railway police work cannot be confined within district limits, and such a restriction will become more and more impossible with the growth of the use of railways by the criminal classes. The Commission, therefore, recommend the general adoption of the provincial system, subject to the proviso that a separate force is unnecessary in the case of provinces . . . In Madras and Burma a change has been made within recent years from the district to the provincial system and in both provinces there was very definite evidence of the beneficial results that have North West Frontier Province which contain only short lengths of line running in from outside; and subject also to the necessity of allowing a departure from the principle in respect of lines running through Native States, which must continue under arrangements similar to those now subsisting. . . . The primary duty of a railway police is the preservation of law and order, but in a few cases they also under take the watch and ward of railway property. The latter practice is condemned by the majority of police officers and railway officials, and the Commission are unable to urge anything in favour of it. The custody of private property is the duty of the owner, and there are no grounds for making any distinction between a railway company and any other private owner. There are obvious objections to entrusting the guardianship of private property to persons over whom the owner has no authority, and these objections have additional force in the case under consideration, as the relations between the company's servants and the police are certain to be still further strained by such a position of dual responsibility for railway property.

By the 1890s, security issues in the railways had become a serious concern, which is why the Indian Police Commission examined the issue of railway policing in such detail. In 1904, a joint commission was formed to investigate inter-provincial crime on the railways in Bengal, the United Provinces and Assam, and found that railway theft was a serious matter. The East Indian, Oudh and Rohilkhand, and Bengal and North-Western Railways were identified as vital lines used by criminals to get the stolen property out of Eastern UP and into Bengal and Assam. The railway lines in Rajputana were the most challenging, from the jurisdictional point of view. There was an issue of sovereignty across all the princely states.[122] The timeline requires more explanation. It was in 1854 that the EIRC first employed some staff and called them 'police', though the Police Act of 1861 had not yet been passed. Once the Police Act of 1861 had been passed, the government of India possessed its own police, and a contingent of this was deployed for the security of the railways. The railway company, often private, bore

---

[122] David A. Campion, 'Railway Policing and Security in Colonial India, c. 1860-1930', in Roopa Srinivasan, Manish Tiwari and Sandeep Silas edited, *Our Indian Railway, Themes in India's Railway History*, Foundation Books, 2006.

75 per cent of the costs, and the government bore the remainder. In 1882, all police on railways were formally classed under 'government police' and 'private police', the latter being employed by companies. The railway companies were thus directly responsible for the protection and security of passengers, property and goods, and they started employing 'chowkidars'. Thus it continued, until the Railway Police (Thomson) Committee of 1921. More accurately, this Committee was established in 1907 and submitted its report in 1921. Since incidents of crime were increasing, this committee recommended that the chowkidari system should be reorganized. The system metamorphosed into a watch-and-ward system, and post-Independence, became the Railway Protection Force (RPF). Many people think RPF stands for Railway Police Force. It doesn't. The relevant 'police' for railways is the GRP (Government Railway Police). The RPF is a security force. Through the ministry of railways, it is under the control of the Union government. You don't become 'police' until you are recognized under the 1861 Police Act. Law and order is a state subject, and the GRP is under the control of state governments, though following the earlier practice, the Indian Railways bears 50 per cent of the costs of the GRP.

Hargrave Lee Adam was a crime writer from the early twentieth century (he was born in 1867) distinctive for writing only about real-life crime. He wrote extensively on such diverse topics as Burke and Hare, the trial of George Henry Lamson, Pritchard the poisoner, and other real-life crime stories. Having written extensively on crime in the western world, he decided to turn eastwards, and the first book he produced after this was *Oriental Crime*, published in 1908. The information was gathered entirely from talking to British civil servants. The second such book was specific to India and was titled *The Indian Criminal*.[123] The information for this too was obtained in a similar way. Its preface said, 'This work has been compiled mainly from verbal and documentary information from various sources, vouchsafed me by gentlemen who have spent many years in the East in administrative capacities; also from information derived from officials still actively engaged in India, and who have been good enough to place themselves in communication with me.' Published in 1909, this had two chapters on thieves operating on the railways.

Adam divided the railway thief into seven classes: (1) The Bhamptas of the Deccan; (2) The Ina Koravars, alias Alagaries, of southern India; (3) The Bharwars of Gonda and Lallatpur; (4) The Mullahs of Muttra; (5) The Bhatrajas or Bhattu Turakas of India; (6) The Takku Woddars or Guntichores of southern India; and (7) The railway pickpockets of India. He also added the 'Indian railway servant' to the list. The Indian railway servant did not generally find favourable mention; trust and responsibility were vested in English railway servants, typically guards and engine-drivers: 'One might add to these another class,

---

[123] *The Indian Criminal*, Hargrave Lee Adam, J. Milne, London, 1909.

consisting of railway servants themselves, although they are not, like those mentioned above, hereditary criminals. They are, however, very daring thieves, and give the authorities a great deal of trouble.'

And, contrary to our earlier statement on guards and engine-drivers, Adam wrote: 'As already mentioned, the railway servants themselves also commit thefts, and give the authorities a deal of trouble. Guards, porters, and even station-masters engage in these thefts, mostly of goods in transit.' This remarkable book mentions the modus operandi of each of these categories of thieves and also their antecedents. He also tried to decode their lingo, specifically, the code language used by the Ina Koravars. In his opinion, the groups from the Deccan, southern India, Gonda and Lallatpur were the most skilful and deceitful. Table 3 has a sample of the lingo decoded by Adam.

If you are wondering about the south India emphasis, that's because Adam didn't get all his information from civil servants, retired or otherwise. He also got it from a book he mentions in the preface. This was a book by M. Paupa Rao Naidu.[124] Like Adam, Paupa Rao Naidu had broader interests. Some of the books he wrote were *The History of Professional Poisoners and Coiners of India*, *The History of Korawars, Erukulas or Kaikaries* and *The History of Bauris, Sansis, Chapperbands, Cabulees and Iranies*.

---

[124] *The History of Railway Thieves, with Hints on Detection*, 3rd edition, 1904. This was published by Higginbotham's.

Table 3: Secret lingo of the professional thief

Secret terms in the native language	Translation in English
Valan, Mooli, Nayi	Policeman
Pothaku	Carpet or canvas bag, or bundle
Polambi	Gold Jewel
Vadayan	Soon
Vasare	Bring
Voru Kuppu	Give arrack
Kulambu	Toddy
Shadayan	Cloth
Boothi	Children
Chalamuti	Necklace
Varipuda	Leave him
Vangittuvanthan	Previously convicted
Keppather	Do not give out your residence
Shadayan irchiti ippico	There is a cloth, take

Some crimes attracted a lot of attention, particularly from the media. This was the case with H. Shugis, who was adviser to the Japanese-British Exhibition of 1910. On 17 April 1911, the *Statesman* newspaper condemned the laxity of railway security.

A Japanese, Mr H. Shugis, adviser to the Japanese-British Exhibition of 1910, was travelling between Arrah and Dinapore. He was the victim of an extensive robbery while travelling as a first class passenger on the East Indian Railway, between Arrah and Dinapore. Mr Shugis appears to have fallen asleep and awoke at the latter place to find that his hand-bag, containing promissory notes and cash and jewellery, amounting to nearly Rs 3,000 was missing. Among the articles stolen, were a solid gold watch and chain, a valuable star sapphire gold ring, several gold scarf pins and brooches, and Rs 700 in promissory notes. Also a gilt pin with the Japanese flag engraved and a gilt and enamel badge of his Japanese Commission as adviser to the Japanese-British Exhibition. The former is said to be a present from the Japanese Government. Despite a vigorous police inquiry, and the offer of a handsome reward for any information that will lead to the arrest of the culprits or the recovery of the stolen property, no clue has so far been obtained.[125]

The Japanese-British Exhibition was held in London between May and October 1910, so it is not very obvious what H. Shugis was doing in India.

But the most celebrated trial with respect to murders committed on trains at the time was what came to be known as the G.I.P. Railway Murder Case. This became a celebrated story because the accused were an Englishman and a Eurasian. The case was tried in the Bombay High Court, and it is best to state the facts in the words used in

---

[125] http://www.irfca.org/articles/clips/running-train-theft-1911.html

the reportage of that time, in 1921.[126] However, we will skip the bits about Morris's first crime, since that was about the Customs and had nothing to do with the railways.

The descent into hell is easy. This famous maxim of Virgil is forcibly illustrated by the criminal career of the principal culprit in what is known as the G.I.P. Railway Murder Case. Two men were put up for trial on a charge of murder at the Criminal Sessions of the Bombay High Court in November 1921 before Mr. Justice Marten and a special jury. One of the two accused was a Eurasian named Morris, and the other was a young Englishman named Donnison. Morris was at one time Baggage Inspector in the Bombay Customs. His duty was to examine and search the baggage of persons arriving by boat and disembarking at the Ballard Pier, to see if they contained any contraband goods. But that was some time ago. At the time of the murders, Morris was apparently without any job and in impecunious circumstances. Donnison, the other accused, also appeared to be a waster without any settled job, although at the time of the murder, he was working in a motor-garage in Bombay.

The two men were charged with having committed the double murder of a pay-clerk and a peon in the employ of G.I.P. Railway Co. These

[126] http://bombayhighcourt.nic.in/libweb/historicalcases/cases/
G_I_P__RAILWAY_MURDER_CASE-1921.html

men were travelling from Bombay in charge of a box containing money in cash and currency notes, which was being carried by train to an upcountry station. According to the prosecution, while the train was proceeding from Igatpuri onwards, the two accused forced an entry into the compartment in which the pay-clerk and the peon were travelling with the cash-box. It was late at night while the train was in motion between two stations. According to the prosecution, Morris and Donnison first smashed the head of the poor peon. Gagging him, and tying up his hands and feet, they left him in a pool of blood on the floor of the compartment. They also attacked the pay-clerk and similarly smashed his head by giving him several blows with a wooden club. A jemmy was also used. They then forced open the money-box and transferred the money from the box into a canvas bag which they had with them. The box contained Rs. 36,000 and odd in currency notes and coin. The murderers took all the currency notes amounting to about Rs. 32,000 and left the rest of the money, about Rs. 4,000 and odd, it being in coin. They then closed the compartment and went back to their own compartment and travelled on until the train reached Manmad the next morning at about 8 or 9 o'clock.

In the meanwhile, early in the morning of 20th of July 1921, the murder was discovered at a way-side station, Pachora. The railway staff and railway police were immediately informed. They appeared on the scene and the compartment in which the murders were committed with the bodies of the victims was detached; and the train was allowed to proceed. The two murderers alighted at Manmad with the canvas bag; and walking along the railway track, buried the canvas bag in a nullah covered with bushes at some distance from the railway station. They then returned, Morris going to Igatpuri where he was residing, and Donnison came down to Bombay.

It appeared that Morris was fairly well known to the station staff at various stations as also to guards and engine drivers on the line from Igatpuri to Deolali. The railway police made vigorous inquiries at the stations and in the railway quarters at Igatpuri. The inquiries showed that for several days preceding the murders, Morris had been observed loitering along the line, and keeping a watch on the through night trains from Bombay at Deolali, as if on the look-out for something or somebody. His movements prior to the crime had excited the curiosity if not the suspicion of the station staff at Deolali. It appeared that on the fatal night of the 19th of July, Morris along with another European had purchased two first class tickets to Manmad, and boarded the train by which the pay-clerk and the peon were travelling. As a result of the investigations made at Deolali, Manmad and Igatpuri, Morris was arrested about the beginning of August, while he was watching a cricket match at Deolali. He was questioned as regards his movements on the night of 19th/20th July. He saw that the game was up; and practically confessed his part in the transaction to the police. He was taken to Manmad, and he pointed out the spot where the money bag and the jemmy were buried. Two days later, on information given by him, Donnison was arrested at his residence at Colaba in Bombay.

After his return to Bombay, having recklessly run through the greater part of the 32,000 rupees,[127] Morris's mind constantly dwelt upon the magnificent time which he had in Europe. He found no job. Very likely he never tried for any honest job, and employed himself in loafing and looking out for some such other windfall as the devil had thrown in his way in the past. The prospect and the taste of poisoned pleasures, purchased with stolen money, ultimately suggested the crime, which brought Morris to the gallows. To replenish his depleted resources and repeat the course of vicious pleasures, which he had once tasted with the gains of robbery, he hunted for some other victim whom he might rob; and the Devil, always at the elbow of seekers after sinful pleasures, pointed to him the pernicious path of dalliance and dissipation through a terrible crime. Morris's search for another easy haul of unearned money at last centered upon the pay-clerks of the G.I.P. Railway, constantly travelling from Bombay with money boxes in their charge. He thought out the plan of

---

[127] From the first crime.

robbery, secured a willing assistant in Donnison; and the two miscreants proceeded to accomplish their bloody business on the fateful night of 19/20 July 1921.

At the trial of the two accused before Mr. Justice Marten and a special jury in November 1921, Morris was ably defended by V.F. Vicajee, a well-known criminal lawyer of the time; and Kenneth Kemp defended Donnison. But the evidence against them was overwhelming; and counsel could do little in the face of such cogent and clear evidence. Both were found guilty. It was a cold-blooded, calculated, preplanned murder from the meanest of all motives. Morris was sentenced to death, and he was ultimately hanged. His companion in crime, Donnison, was sentenced to penal servitude for life in view of his youth, and the fact that he had participated in the murders under the dominating influence of Morris, who had planned the whole transaction.

A very curious coincidence of the two crimes committed by Morris was the fact that the amount of money which he secured by cheating, robbery and murder on the two occasions was about the same, viz. Rs. 32,000. Another very striking feature of the case is the sinister role of the notorious number 13 in this bloody business. The train by which the ill-fated clerk and peon travelled on their last journey on earth, was the 13 Down Passenger Train from Bombay to Jubbulpore; and the number of the carriage, which contained the compartment of death, was 3613. This was noted by Mr. Justice Marten in his admirable summing up to the jury. Apart from the last '13' in '3613' the total of the digits $(3 + 6 + 1 + 3)$ also comes to 13. It is such coincidences that keep alive ancient superstitions and give them a fresh vitality; and facts, on occasions, are stranger than fiction.

We have already mentioned the inferior treatment meted out to Indians on the railways. This naturally had a ramification on nationalist politics and the non-cooperation movement.[128] Especially during the closing decades of the nineteenth century, the development of the railways fed into the nationalist movement. The most obvious aspect of it was the way Indians were treated on the railways. But there was also the discrimination faced by Indian workers on the railway system. The early economic nationalists, like Dadabhai Naoroji, Ganesh Vyankatesh Joshi and G. Subramania Iyer, also flagged the non-profitability of railway lines and the failure of the railways to bring about an industrial revolution along the lines of what Karl Marx had anticipated.[129] The first organized strike in the railways was in the Jamalpur workshop in 1919. A quotation illustrates what this was all about.

The British railways in colonial India had a twofold contradictory identity, to the British they were a

---

[128] See, Campion, *op. cit.*

[129] See, Bipan Chandra, 'Economic Nationalism and the Railway Debate, circa 1880-1905', in Roopa Srinivasan, Manish Tiwari and Sandeep Silas, *op.cit.*

symbol of the Raj but to the Indian mind they had come to signify its opposite—the colonial reality, its exploitation, humiliation and the imperial arrogance of the 'ferenghi'. By 1919 the native workmen had come to be alienated from their work by the tensions created due to the racial discrimination in the labour process. As the superior grades of railway workmen were whites, it was left to the 'peripheral' categories of Indian railwaymen—the drivers and guards of goods trains, unimportant station masters of the small stations, the 'native' firemen travelling a long time on a British train in the shadow of a 'ferenghi' driver, the signallers and the workshop men—to assert rights through various forms of popular protests.[130]

During the Quit India Movement, the Andhra Provincial Congress Committee issued instructions to all its district Congress committees, prescribing six distinct stages of action. One of these stages included stopping trains by pulling chains and travelling without tickets.[131] The Civil Disobedience Movement interfaced with the railways, and there was also an interface of the railways with the violent strands of the freedom struggle. The Kakori

---

[130] Pushpa Kumari, 'The Gandhian Movement and Railway Workers in Bihar: A Case Study of the Workers of Jamalpur Railway Workshop (1919-1930)', *The NEHU Journal*, Vol XIII, No. 2, July-December 2015

[131] Lisa Mitchell, 'To stop train pull chain: Writing histories of contemporary political practice', *Indian Economic and Social History Review*, October/December 2011 48: 469–495.

Conspiracy or Kakori Train Robbery was one example of this. On 9 August 1925, this robbery was organized by the Hindustan Republican Association. The facts are known to everyone and need not be repeated. The 8 Down Train from Shahjahanpur to Lucknow was looted when it approached Kakori station. Rs 8,000 was seized from the money-bag in the guard's cabin. Pandit Ram Prasad Bismil was one of the founder members of the Hindustan Republican Association and was also involved in planning the Kakori Train Robbery. He is was also a poet and song writer, credited with penning some unforgettable lines, such as '*mera rang de basanti chola*' and '*sarfaroshi ki tamanna ab hamaare dil mein hai*'.

Courtesy IRFCA

There were other such incidents too, like the 'Viceregal train outrage' of 23 December 1929, when Lord Irwin's train was returning to Delhi and, near Humayun's tomb, a bomb exploded on the tracks, causing minor damage[132] (the dining car was destroyed). In 1940, the train between Khalispur and Babatpur was stopped and the mail van looted, and so on.

When India became independent in 1947, the railways' evolution since the 1830s left a complicated legacy, which we have sought to depict anecdotally. That's the reason why we still have the Indian Railway Companies Act of 1895 on the statute books. This is 'An Act to provide for the payment by Railway Companies registered under the Indian Companies Act, 1882, of interest out of capital during construction.' When one hears of the Indian Railways paying 'dividends' to the government of India through Railway Convention Committees, the antecedents go back to the Indian Railway Companies Act of 1895.

Though this book ends with 15 August 1947, the Railway Budget speeches of those immediate post-Independence years illustrate the state the Indian railway network was in.

The Transport Member, introducing the Railway Budget for 1947–48 on 27 February 1947, said:

> With the management of Government owned railways passing into the hands of Government the problem of regrouping them into convenient units for more efficient management has assumed greater importance. Accordingly this matter has

---
[132] *Ibid.*

been considered afresh and while Government are alive to the necessity for taking up this question at the earliest possible moment, they feel that for two reasons no firm decision in this regard can be taken in the immediate future. Firstly, the railways have not yet recovered from the effects of war, and any, attempt at regrouping at this stage would tend to throw the organisation out of gear to such an extent as to hamper rapid rehabilitation. Secondly, several new line constructions and restorations of dismantled lines are under investigation and any decision on regrouping would be premature until the investigations are completed and a decision is taken as to which of the projects are finally to be taken in hand.[133]

Dr John Mathai introduced the Railway Budget for 1948–49 on 24 February 1948.

Firstly, there is this very obvious fact that we have come to the end of the period of serious civil disturbances. We have come to the end of these vast refugee movements. The House will remember that altogether during a period of two-and-a-half months the Railways were called upon to move as many as 3 million refugees, which represents the

---

[133] http://www.indianrailways.gov.in/railwayboard/uploads/
directorate/finance_budget/Previous%20Budget%20
Speeches/1947-48.pdf

capacity of a thousand passenger trains. That was
a terrible strain on the Railways and we have now
come to the end of that period of strain. Secondly,
I told the House last November that one of the
problems we are faced with—have been faced with
since the end of the war—is the large diversion of
traffic which has occurred as the result of various
war developments. A large volume of traffic is
now moving along routes which are not equipped
for dealing with this large amount of traffic and I
said therefore that it would be necessary for us to
consider the question of improving and extending
our marshalling yards, that is to say, those yards
where you distribute wagons with reference to
their ultimate destination . . . Next I will deal
with the difficulties that arose from the transfer
and exchange of staff between India and Pakistan.
That was a factor which led to a very great deal
of disorganization on the Railways, about 100,000
men being exchanged and settled in new positions
in the course of about 2½ months. Now that
general dislocation is rapidly disappearing and
men are beginning to settle down in their new
positions. But one of the most serious difficulties
that we had to face was that this transfer resulted
on our side in a shortage of essential workers in
particular categories. The House will remember
that where the most serious difficulty arose
on this account was the East Indian Railway in
regard to their engine crew, which created, as I

said, a first-class national crisis in respect of coal movements.[134]

On 23 February 1949, it was N. Gopalaswami Ayyangar who introduced the Railway Budget for 1949–50.

With the conditions that prevailed in the country immediately after the transfer of power in 1947 and the manner in which Railways had to function under those conditions, the House has been made fully familiar by my predecessor when he introduced the Budgets for the later 7 months of 1947–48 and for the year 1948–49. I do not propose to deal with them again on this occasion. The strain of the second world war, the splitting into two of a united railway system, the violent civil disturbances in the Punjab, the aggression and fighting in Kashmir, the Hyderabad Police action, the general economic and transport upset— these and other similar developments in the country confronted the Railway Administrations with problems at once difficult, grave and unprecedented in their nature and intensity . . . Hon'ble Members are, I know, greatly interested in the problem of the re-grouping of railways in this country. Amongst the 9 units of Railway

---

[134] http://www.indianrailways.gov.in/railwayboard/uploads/ directorate/finance_budget/Previous%20Budget%20 Speeches/1948-49.pdf

Administrations now in existence, the route mileage in charge of each varies from 1,231 miles on the Assam Railway to 4,457 miles on the E.I. Railway. Their operation ratios vary within fairly wide limits and some of them have been living on the others. Their present geographical distribution has grown haphazardly in some cases and are a product of the history of both State and Company effort in the past. Whether we should interfere with the present grouping at all and, if so, how best to group them with the assurance of giving satisfaction both territorially and functionally is a problem which bristles with difficulties. The Railway Board and I are studying this problem in all its various aspects. The dimensions of the problem change daily. The political developments in Indian States and Unions of Indian States are at present a disturbing factor in the way of arriving at conclusions which can have any permanence. When, however, the political map of India gets finally settled, as there is every prospect of its doing in the very near future, we should be in a position to re-draw the railway map of India and cut it up into units of Railway Administration, which will ensure both regional and operational efficiency.[135]

---

[135] http://www.indianrailways.gov.in/railwayboard/uploads/ directorate/finance_budget/Previous%20Budget%20 Speeches/1949-50.pdf

The present nationalized system of Indian Railways (IR) would come into being soon. However, despite the nationalization, there was left a rather odd and anomalous legacy. The Central Provinces Railway Company (CPRC) which was incorporated in 1910, still runs a private railway network in India. And this isn't one of those railway networks on private estates, plantations, sugar mills, collieries, mines, dams, harbours, ports or steel plants. Nor is it a line that a private company temporarily builds and operates, to be eventually handed over to Indian Railways. Once upon a time, the CPRC used to have other lines, like the Dhond (Daund)–Baramati (opened 1914–15), the Pulgaon–Arvi (opened 1917–18), the Pachora–Jamner (opened 1919) and the Darwha–Pusad (opened 1931). These became part of IR, continued as narrow gauge and remained neglected lines or were wound up (Darwha–Pusad). The only exception is the strange case of the Ellichpur–Murtazapur–Yeotmal Railway, owned by the CPRC and known as the Shakuntala Railway. Murtazapur (Akola district) is in Maharashtra and is a junction in the Bhusawal division of the Central Railway (CR), along the main Mumbai–Nagpur–Howrah broad gauge line. However, a narrow gauge line also passes through Murtazapur, divided into a seventy-six km northern stretch between Murtazapur and Achalpur/Ellichpur and a 113-km south-eastern stretch between Murtazapur and Yeotmal/Yavatmal. The Yavatmal stretch was opened in 1903, and the Achalpur stretch in 1913. Both segments were constructed and operated by GIPR. In 1925, the GIPR became part of IR. Therefore, IR started to operate a narrow gauge train along the Shakuntala Railway (the train is known as the Shakuntala Express). Locomotives were initially steam, replaced with diesel in 1995. What is unique about the Shakuntala Railway is that the track is still owned by a private company while the trains are run by IR (meaning the CR). Since the GIPR was only an operator, who owns the Shakuntala Railway? Killick Nixon (set up in 1857), the agent for the CPRC, does, though Killick Nixon has now moved from British to Indian hands. But there was still a contract between the CPRC and the CR for this line. CPRC was eventually 'nationalized' in 2016.

The locomotive once used for the Shakuntala Express

Incidentally, in 1949, India borrowed for the railways from the International Bank for Reconstruction and Development/World Bank. The bank's report, appraising India's loan application, makes for interesting reading.

Since India does not at present manufacture locomotives and tank wagons, to correct the shortage of motive power, the Indian Railways began placing orders late in 1947 for 863 locomotives, spare boilers, and spare parts from the USA, Canada, the United Kingdom, and France . . . The goal is to reduce the locomotive fleet from the present figure of more than 7,000 engines to 6,000 engines within the next 10 years. Accordingly, lines which receive new engines are required to scrap old engines in return, at a ratio varying from 12 to 17 new engines for every 10 new engines delivered.[136]

On India's behalf, this loan agreement was signed (on 18 August 1949) by Vijaya Lakshmi Pandit, then Indian ambassador to the USA.

Such has been the fascinating story of the evolution of the Indian railway network, from its early beginnings in the 1830s! We hope you enjoyed reading it as much as we enjoyed telling it. Indian Railways is now in the midst of structural reform. Those reforms are based on the recommendations of several committees, including the one that was mentioned in the preface,[137] and involve changing several elements that were part of the historical evolution we have described.

---

[136] Loan document from the World Bank, archives accessed by the authors.

[137] *Report of the Committee for Mobilization of Resources for Major Railway Projects and Restructuring of Railway Ministry and Railway Board*, Ministry of Railways, June 2015.